Simone Siesto

Forex: The Holy Grail

Simone Siesto was born in Porto Torres, Italy.

He graduated in Economics, at the Università degli Studi di Sassari at the age of 23. Since the age of 20, he started trading in European and US markets, including stock indices, cfd, individual stocks, and currency (forex) markets. He is an author for financial websites offering a variety of market analyses and trading instructions. Over 15 years of work in trading, he devised new proprietary indicators and expert advisor for swing and position trading. He decided to gather his experience and knowledge in the book: forex-the holy grail.

To my parents, Andrea and Silvana.

With love.

Copyright © 2016. All rights reserved. Except for quotations, no part of this book may be reproduced or transmitted in any form or by any other means, electronic or mechanical, including photocopying, recording, uploading to the Internet, or by any information storage and retrieval system, without a written permission from Dr. Simone Siesto.

DISCLAIMER

By using the information within this book, you agree that it is general educational material and you will not hold anybody responsible for loss or damages resulting from the content provided here. Spot currency trading have large potential rewards but also large potential risk. You must be aware of the risks and be willing to accept them in order to invest in the futures, options or currency markets. Don't trade with money you can't afford to lose. This book is neither a solicitation nor an offer to buy/sell currencies. No representation is being made that any account will or is likely to achieve profits or losses similar to those discussed on this website or in any of its material. The past performances of any trading system or methodology is not necessarily indicative of future results.

Contents

1. Outlook

"I have never met a rich technician" - *Jim Rogers.*

"I always laugh at people who say: "I've never met a rich technician". I love that! It's such an arrogant, nonsensical response. I used fundamentals for 9 years and got rich as a technician" -*Marty Schwartz.*

26 July 2012, London.

In the midst of the debt crisis that was gripping a collapsing euro zone in 2011, amid the surging yield bonds, the President of the European Central Bank Mario Draghi said a few words that became famous: "*Whatever it takes to preserve the Euro*". The speech at the press conference had a great resonance worldwide and even lay people are now aware how monetary policies can affect the lives of each one of us. The forex (foreign exchange market) is an over-the counter market for the trading of currencies. It is open twenty-four hours per day and five days per week. It is the largest market in terms of traded volumes in the world, with an estimated turnover of five trillion of Us Dollars per day. National central banks along with international banks and hedge funds are the main players involved in Forex trading. Over the recent years, due also to intensive advertising on the web, Forex gained a great popularity, acquiring an increasing number of retail traders.

So, why a book entitled: "Forex- the Holy Grail"? The Holy Grail is a myth; the quest to find it, that of the Chalice with the blood of Christ is a story shrouded in legend, one that moved imaginations and energies since the high Middle Ages. In particular, the word "Grail" seems to come from the French language. In fact, "Graal" should mean "cup" or "dish". According to the medieval legend, the "Holy Grail" is the cup from which Jesus Christ drank during the "Last Supper" and some scholars of medieval literature identify that cup with the same cup that Joseph of Arimathea used to collect his blood, from the wound inflicted by Longinus's spear. The cup, immediately the first and forever the most coveted relic in Christianity, was then taken to England through Europe, laying the foundation for much of the Arthurian cycle of the Knights of the Round Table, as well as many other stories. The quest for the Grail, as undertaken by many a brave knight, would be a long, arduous journey, fraught with dangers and temptations for the body and the soul. The rewards, almost unattainable by definition, would be atonement for sins, healing, communion with the divine and even immortality.

The main objective of this book is then to guide the reader through a similar quest for the elusive "Holy Grail" in Forex, providing everything the reader needs to find out where the "Holy Grail" may be. There are different ways to make a profit in forex, just as there are different opinions as to where the "Holy Grail" might be. Different personalities, backgrounds and life experiences obviously led to different results. In order to guide the reader along this challenging quest, the author develops a methodology that any trader can implement, regardless of the level of experience in trading forex.

In the search for the "Holy Grail" in Forex, an important distinction is made between fundamental and technical analysis. Over the years, experts have debated over which methodology might be more profitable. The first section of the book focuses on the technical analysis and, in particular, on the investigation and the evaluation of some classic indicators and price patterns, to verify their ability to generate profits in the current markets. The second part focuses instead on the study of the fundamental analysis, which is a way to predict a currency's future performance through the study of macroeconomic variables, such as the gross domestic product, the inflation rate, the interest rate or the unemployment rate. Later in the book, the author explores how a number of sophisticated trading systems perform over the time, concluding that some of them might perform well for a currency pair, but they might be not profitable for other ones. It is therefore essential to identify common trading rules to be applied to different currency pairs. In the final section, the reader will learn how to manage a trade, how to scale in or scale out and where to target the profits. This is the "Money Management" section. Since every trade can result in a loss or in a profit, what makes a big difference is the way a trade is managed. In general, a good trader has the ability to manage different trades using tested and repetitive strategies, rather than predicting future movements for every single trade. In this sense, the author shows how, poor money management leads to final losses, even if the profitable trades are six or seven out of ten.

What beginners will find surprising is that there is a concrete possibility to trade the correct market direction less than fifty percent of the time, and yet to still make a profit.

"The Holy Grail! —

... What is it?

The phantom of a cup that comes and goes?"

Alfred, Lord Tennyson

2. Forex is about probabilities

"The only function of economic forecasting is to make astrology look respectable"-

John Kenneth Galbraith

It is not easy to be consistently profitable over time. Statistics suggest that ninety percent of the retail traders eventually lose money. Unfortunately, it is not possible to close every trade with a profit; for this reason, many traders are tempted to close the profitable ones too early, and leave the negative ones open, as they are unwilling to accept a loss, hoping that they will turn to profits in a near future. This way of trading is normally not profitable, especially if it does not take in account hedging a trade. "Hedging" is undoubtedly an important tool in the search of the "Holy Grail" in Forex. In fact, a good hedging enables traders to get higher profits than those resulted from a one-direction type of trading. Further on, it is explained how a classic way of hedging consists of triggering a long trade on a currency pair and shorting another one, when between the two cross pairs there is a high correlation and the first pair is showing a relative strength greater than the second. At any rate, before analyzing how hedging works, it is appropriate to understand that Forex is a matter of probabilities. There is a fifty percent of possibilities to be wrong or right, since a currency can move up or down. This scenario implies two questions: How should a trader manage a profitable or a losing trade? What is the right time to take a profit or a loss? With that in mind, it is appropriate to stress that like in every other market, each time a trader buys or sells a currency pair, a counterpart does exactly the opposite, so it is not advisable to become too attached to a trade. Furthermore, every trader should always have a trading plan before placing any kind of trade. What can make a trading plan profitable is the ability to stop the losses while they are still small enough to be managed. Essentially, the ability of a profitable trader is to close several positions with a small loss and to let the winning ones run. The following hypothetical scenario might help to clarify this concept. A trader plans to trade with $ 10.000 and to divide the amount in ten micro lots of $ 1000 each. The trader closes seven winning trades out of ten, and accepts a profit of fifty dollars for each winning trade and a loss of one hundred dollars for each of the remaining three trades. Under these conditions, the result is a gain of $ 50, since the winning trades generate $ 350, while the three losing trades lead to a loss of $ 300. If the trader is profitable six times out of ten, however, using the same risk/rewards ratio, the trade would generate a loss of one hundred dollars. What if the trade generates an equal number of profitable and losing trades? The outcome is a loss of $ 250! These examples clarify how a strategy with a risk/reward ratio of 2:1 is a losing one. It is never recommendable to implement a trading plan using this risk/reward ratio, since it requires being accurate most of the times. On the long run, the market would take down the trader. It is then recommended to use at least a 1:1 risk/reward ratio. If a trader looks for a 50 dollars of profit, the cutting point for losses should never be more than 50 dollars as well. Professional traders focus on managing their position in an appropriate manner. They usually look for a potential profit at least twice the loss. In the hypothetical scenario from above, and assuming an equal number of winning and losing trades and a loss of $ 50, the outcome would be a $250 profit, proving that money management makes the difference. In other words, what makes the difference is how a trader handles different positions in terms of profit or loss. Next chapter illustrates what a trend is, how to recognize it and how to exploit it for generating profitable trades.

"Avoid the Holy Grail, the heroic journeys, the pursuit of a legend--
that is not the life of the bookaneer, who must keep his eyes on the ground
while other book people live by dreaming."

Matthew Pearl, *The Last Bookaneer*

3. Trend. Definition and how to detect it

"Don't try to buy at the bottom or sell at the top" - *Bernard Baruch*

A currency, or in general, a stock, is trending when is moving in the same direction on a given time period. More specifically, an uptrend is a series of higher-highs and higher- lows (Chart 1), while a downtrend is a series of lower-highs and lower-lows (Chart 2).

The following charts show an uptrend and, conversely, a downtrend.

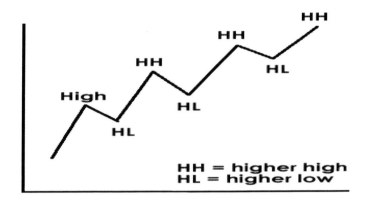

Chart 1. Uptrend

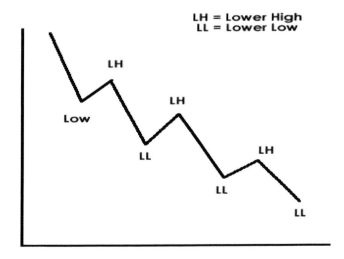

Chart 2. Downtrend

Having defined what a trend is, and how it can be recognized, we shall discuss how to trade a trend. On the web, finding enthusiastic feedbacks about how to exploit a profitable trend is quite easy. Unfortunately, some brokers try to attract clients and limit the instructions to a couple of lessons about trends and claim that everyone can trade in forex. However, there is a vested reason why they do it. The greater number of traders in the market, the larger their profits. What most of people do not know is that real trading works differently. Forex trading needs time, expertise, studies and patience.

Undoubtedly, following a trend offers the opportunity to be with the price, and statistically there are more chances of closing a position with a profit. It is exactly like surfing a wave or sailing: You need a strong wind. In theory, it seems easy but, unfortunately, a trend might reverse at any time. Furthermore, while promoting this method, some brokers often forget to point out that a trend is known only once it is already formed, and never before. As shown above, forming an uptrend requires a sequence of higher-highs and higher-lows, while a downtrend requires a sequence of lower-highs and lower-lows. However, what if the price starts moving randomly? While a trader waits for the formation of a trend, the price might suddenly change direction, causing a loss. Since the markets are not always in trend, being profitable in the forex is not easy. Statistics report that the markets move in trend about the 30% of the time. This means they move in a range or in a more erratic way for the other 70%. The next chapter will illustrate different ways of trading using trend-following systems.

Holy Grail rule number 1:

An uptrend is a series of higher-highs and higher-lows. A downtrend is a series of lower-highs and lower-lows. Once an uptrend is detected, a trader can trigger a long position at the break of the previous high. Once a downtrend is detected, a trader can trigger a short position at the break of the previous low.

"You see, he was going for the Holy Grail. The boys all took a flier at the Holy Grail now and then. It was a several years' cruise. They always put in the long absence snooping around, in the most conscientious way, though none of them had any idea where the Holy Grail really was, and I don't think any of them actually expected to find it, or would have known what to do with it if he had run across it."

Mark Twain, A Connecticut Yankee in King Arthur's Court

4. Choosing a time frame

"The markets are the same now as they were five or ten years ago because they keep changing just like they did then"- *Ed Seykota*

Once learned how to recognize a trend, it is necessary to analyze a specific time frame. In order to succeed in such analysis, however, a trader should recall that to each currency pair corresponds an indefinite number of trends and that *the longer the period of data analyzed the greater the reliability of the trend.* Trading over short time frames, such as five or fifteen minutes, is often not reliable. The risk is to be a perfect score of your broker, in virtue of the spread and of the paid repricing, especially during the hours with the highest volatility. Trading over short time frames may not be convenient for another simple reason: it is not possible to predict whether a large financial institution or a hedge fund are suddenly placing an order on the market which can generate a movement of a few pips. Moreover, trading short time frames often means trading prices with no concrete direction (choppy prices). On the other hand, trading over longer time frames provides a better view on the *"real trend"* and, at the same time, a concrete understanding of the fight among bulls and bears, in the Forex arena. So it is always advisable to first analyze the monthly and weekly charts and then set up the entries, by using a daily or a four- hour time frame chart. Chart 3 shows the EUR/USD trend on a monthly time frame. This period allows a trader to visualize the overall trend. A clear downtrend is recognizable as a sequence of lower-highs and lower-lows. A virtual channel, with a slightly negative slope, is identified as a virtual projection from the previous highs and lows. In this specific case a smart trader can identify three big trend cycles, dating as far back as 2009. The latest trend is identifiable as of May 2014, when the price started to move downwards, after hitting a virtual resistance at 1.40. The lower section, instead, contains three indicators with a selling signal.

Chart 3.

Created with Prorealtime

Chart 4 provides a closer view on EUR/USD trend on a weekly timeframe. In July 2012, the Euro became stronger against the US Dollar in a smooth sequence of higher-highs and higher-lows. Over two years, the Euro moved from 1.20 to 1.40, while as of May 2014, it began to decline strongly. Both the Macd and the Shaff trend cycle indicators confirm the downtrend, generating a selling signal. Let us now zoom in and analyze the most recent trend by studying the daily chart.

EUR/USD Spot

© www.ProRealTime.com I dati sono forniti a titolo indicativo.

■MACD 12 26 ■MA9

■CCI 20

■Shaff Trend Cycle 10 23 50

Mag Lug Set Nov **2013** Mar Mag Lug Set Nov **2014** Mar Mag Lug Set Nov **2015**

Chart 4

Created with Prorealtime

Chart n. 5 gives an insight into the downtrend, originating in May 2014. A trader should be aware that it is best to trigger only short trades, since in the opposite case, the chances of being profitable decrease dramatically. Once again, it is important to trade only the *main current* trend. However, oftentimes the trend differs for every timeframe analyzed. In this case, a trader can analyze the daily chart, as it shows the most recent price trend, while monitoring those price levels which can be determined from the study of weekly and monthly charts, which may generate a trend reversal.

Chart 5

Created with Prorealtime

In any case, it is always appropriate to trade on those charts that detect a trend clearly and where a multi time frame accordance is recognizable. Trading over shorter timeframes is not recommended unless the trend is in accordance with the weekly or the daily one. Essentially, a trader cannot understand what the *"real main trend"* is, without looking at larger timeframes or, in other words, there is a high probability to trade choppy prices or retracements of the overall trend. Although being profitable is not impossible, timeframes such as five or fifteen minutes are not as reliable as the longer ones. Over the years, traders have developed several expert advisors and performed thousands of tests. The outcome is that different strategies, applied over short time frames, often lead to disappointing performance. In addition, the "spread" fee retail traders pay may cause a repricing, especially during times of increased volatility. The next charts will illustrate other examples of downtrend or uptrends, and other cases where a smooth trend is not recognizable.

Chart 6

Created with Metatrader 5.0

Chart 6 shows how the British Pound moved against the US Dollar over the 2014 on a daily basis: a downtrend is recognizable. It is smooth, with just one relevant retracement in September 2014. In the specific case, traders only look for short trades, as there are not reasons to open long trades.

Chart 7 is instead an example of no trend. It shows how the US Dollar performed against the Turkish Lira on a five-minute time frame. Quotation moved randomly and in the late evening, the price had moved upwards from 2.454 to 2.468: however, during the Asian session, the price just squeezed with no direction and a very low volatility. Finally, in the morning, the quotation dropped to 2.448. The example clarifies how erratic movements make trading on a five-minutes chart a risky business. Chart 8 shows how the British Pound performed against the US Dollar on a fifteen-minutes timeframe. Even in this case, there are no recognizable trends, since there are any higher-highs and higher-lows that can point to an uptrend; similarly, there are no lower-highs and lower-lows to indicate a downtrend.

Chart 7

Created with Prorealtime

The quotation just squeezed between 1.55 and 1.56, respectively the support and the resistance threshold. This is an example of a range chart. In this scenario being profitable is possible only following and trading each small trend inside the range, which is extremely difficult. Not surprisingly, professionals avoid trading in this way, as they rather wait to see where the price is going to move. Only a strong breakout, below 1.548 or above 1.56, may be considered as a valid reason to trigger a trade in the same direction of the breakout. The next example clarifies how it is always better to analyze larger time frames for understanding the underlying trend. Chart n. 9 shows how the Euro traded against the Turkish Lira on a daily time frame over the 2015. The price moved with no direction, generating two false breakouts to the upside and downside, respectively at 3.03 and 2.60. Above 2.90, the bulls have tried to break up the resistance, generating a false breakout. Similarly, below 2.60, the bears have tried to force the support with no success, causing another fake break. Therefore, it is necessary to analyze a different timeframe to understand whether there is a long-term trend, not visible on the daily chart.

Chart 8

Created with Metatrader 5.0

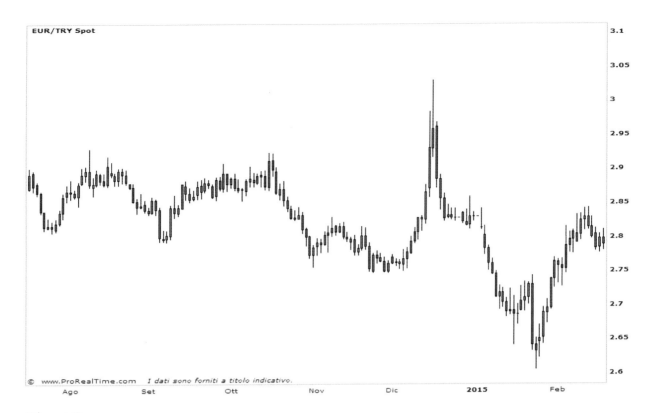

Chart 9

Created with Prorealtime

Chart 10

Created with Prorealtime

Chart 10 shows the same cross on a weekly time frame. A strong uptrend, originated at the beginning of 2013, is now visible. In June, the bullish forces took control of the market, pushing the price higher to form a spike at 3.20; right after that, the bears were finally able to reject it back to 2.60. Technically, these movements formed a price pattern similar to the engulfing bearish one. The latter is a pattern which occurs when a large black candlestick fully engulfs the white candlestick from the period before. It is more effective at the end of a consistent uptrend and it usually forecasts the beginning of a downtrend in the near term. Essentially, the chart from above allows a better understanding about the pair's movements over the last 3 years. In fact, a trader is now aware that an uptrend was in place for 2 years, while, after 2014, the prevailing trend was downward. Chart 11 shows the same cross on a monthly time frame. The reader will notice a multi-year uptrend with a spike formed in January 2014 when, as pointed out earlier, the bearish forces pushed the quotation back to 2.60: the new support threshold. While the weekly chart detects a pattern similar to the engulfing bearish, the monthly one identifies a reversal pinball. It is a bearish pattern that usually occurs at the top of an uptrend. The bulls fail to push the price higher, and the bearish forces are then able to reject it downward. *The longer is the tail of the pin ball, the greater is the effectiveness.* The pinball is followed by a Doji candle, which represents a sign of indecision. The next candle is a black closing Marubozu, which certifies that the bearish forces have finally taken control of the market. The uptrend is still in place; however, the Euro is forecast to hit further highs versus the Turkish Lira, only above the resistance.

Chart 12 shows how the US Dollar moved against the Turkish Lira on a weekly time frame. Throughout 2012 the price moved randomly, with a relative low volatility. On average, the Japanese candles are quite short as noticeable observing the distance between the highs and the lows of each of them. When the volatility tends to fall under its average, it is usually a sign that the market is having a break before the hit of a bigger and explosive movement. This is what happened in June 2013, when a break of the resistance at 1.90 generated a violent movement upward.

EUR/TRY Spot

© www.ProRealTime.com   I dati sono forniti a titolo indicativo.

Set 2010 Mag Set 2011 Mag Set 2012 Mag Set 2013 Mag Set 2014 Mag Set 2015

Chart 11

Created with Prorealtime

How a price moves after a breakout can be explained using the laws of physics, and, in particular, measuring the trajectory of the price with the linear regression line. A regression line is a straight line that attempts to predict the relationship between two points, also known as a trend line or line of best fit. Normally when the price breaks the resistance, the angle taken by the slope of the linear regression line becomes bigger. However, when the angle becomes greater than sixty degrees, like at the end of the 2013, a turnaround is predictable. Essentially, the price can hardly continue to move in such a vertical way, as if responding to the law of gravity. In our example, after the break, inertia pushes the US Dollar higher against the Turkish Lira on the same direction as the original one. However, when the angle of the slope of the linear regression becomes too wide, as at the beginning of 2014, it should be expected a reversal.

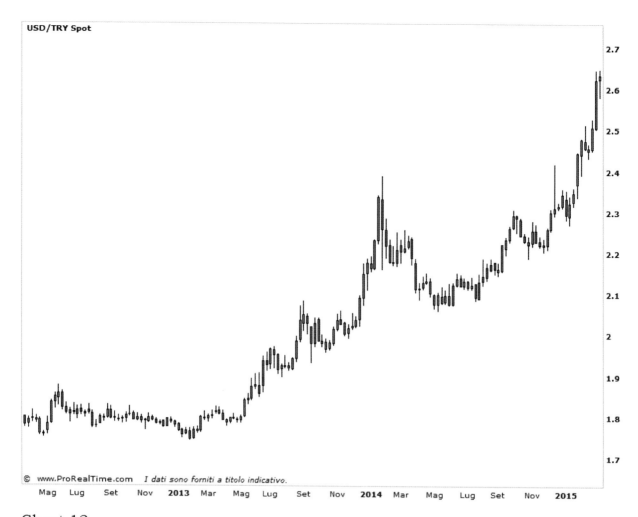

USD/TRY Spot

© www.ProRealTime.com   *I dati sono forniti a titolo indicativo.*

Mag   Lug   Set   Nov   **2013**   Mar   Mag   Lug   Set   Nov   **2014**   Mar   Mag   Lug   Set   Nov   **2015**

Chart 12

Created with Prorealtime

<u>Holy Grail rule number 2:</u>

Do not trade over the shorter timeframes, such as the five or the fifteen-minute ones. *The real trend can be detected only analyzing longer timeframes, as the daily or the weekly ones.* These time-frames provide an effective insight into the fight between bulls and bears.

"The Holy Thing is here again

Among us, brother, fast thou too and pray,

And tell thy brother knights to fast and pray,

That so perchance the vision may be seen

By thee and those, and all the world be healed."

Alfred, Lord Tennyson

5. Strong versus Weak

"Beware of geeks bearing formulas" – Warren Buffet

Most of the traders ignore the balance of power among different currencies. Before studying the most important indicators of technical analysis, it is then necessary to learn how to evaluate the relative strength of one currency compared to another one. The goal is to find which currency shows the higher relative strength within a given time period. This type of analysis enables the trader to buy strong currencies and to sell weak ones. The following study may help understanding the best-performing currencies; it takes into account several currency pairs: Euro/US Dollar (nicknamed "*Fiber*"), the Euro/British Pound ("*Chunnel*"), the British Pound/US Dollar ("*Cable*"), the Australian Dollar/US Dollar ("*Aussie*") and finally, the New Zealand Dollar/US Dollar ("*Kiwi*").

The US Dollar is the dominant reserve currency over the globe. Whenever risk aversion increases, traders tend to buy US Treasuries, which leads to an increased demand for US Dollars. The Euro is the second traded and the second most popular reserve currency in the world. The British Pound is the fourth most traded currency and it is highly traded as a reserve currency, as well. The Australian Dollar, also known as a commodity currency, is the fifth most traded currency in the world. Finally, the New Zealand Dollar, is one of the most ten traded currencies in the world. Firstly, we can compare the Euro with the Sterling and the Greenback (*Sterling* and *Greenback* respectively are the nicknames attributed to the British Pound and to the US Dollar). Chart 13 shows the Fiber trend throughout 2015. The Fiber moved in a stable downtrend, in a sequence of lower-highs and lower-lows, dropping approximatively 16.05 percent. The trend is so smooth that waiting for a retracement before trading would make no sense. Not surprisingly, these kinds of charts are the experienced traders' favorite since the trend is clearly visible and they can trade it without hesitations. Obviously, The Euro is weaker than the Greenback.

Chart 14 shows the Cable trend over the same period of time. As in the Fiber case, the Sterling dropped against the Greenback significantly. In terms of percentage, the Cable lost 10.58 points, which means that the Sterling tumbled less than what the Euro did against the US Dollar. Chart 15 shows the balance of power between the Euro and the Sterling. In 2014, the Chunnel moved within a wide range, testing the resistance several times at approx. 0.80 and the support at 0.78. The consequent breakout of the support decreed the beginning of a smooth downtrend. The difference in terms of performance is simply due to the last three months, when the Euro lost five points against the Pound Sterling. Clearly, this chart shows that the Sterling is stronger than the Euro.

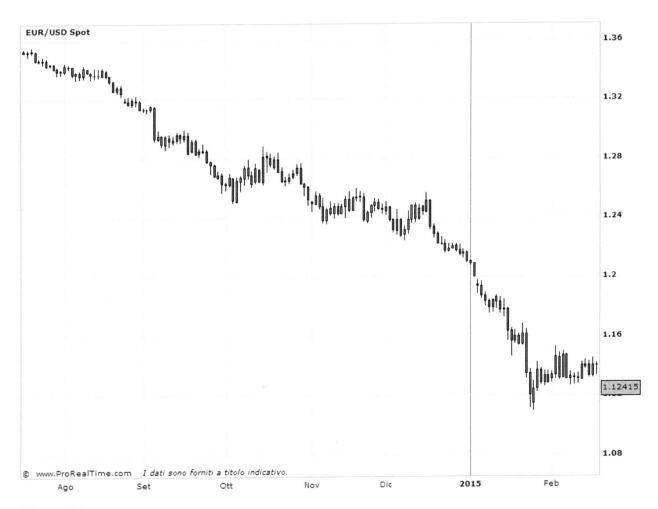

Chart 13

Created with Prorealtime

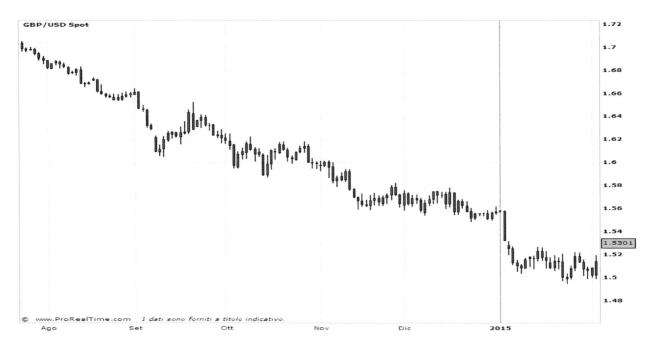

Chart 14

Created with Prorealtime

Chart 15

Created with Prorealtime

Charts 16 and 17 compare the Australian and the New Zealand Dollars to the US Dollar. In particular, chart 16 shows how the Australian Dollar moved against the US Dollar on a daily time frame. Over the period selected, the Aussie fell steadily, with no relevant retracements. Definitely, the relative

29

strength of the Australian Dollar has been significantly lower than the one of the US Dollar. In terms of percentage, the Aussie lost 17 points. Chart 17 shows the kiwi trend. In this case, the downtrend was less pronounced if compared to the Aussie one. In terms of percentage, the variation was approximately 13 points. The US Dollar is definitely the strongest currency over the period selected. The British Pound is the second strongest currency, since it outperforms against the New Zealand Dollar but loses to the Greenback. On the other hand, the weakest currencies are the Euro and the Australian Dollar; in particular, the latter has delivered the worst performance among the five currencies selected. This simple analysis allows the trader to understand what currency is outperforming the others. A smart trader is willing to open long positions on the US Dollar, once the technical analysis suggests it might be the right time to do it.

Holy Grail rule number 3:
Buy strong and sell weak.

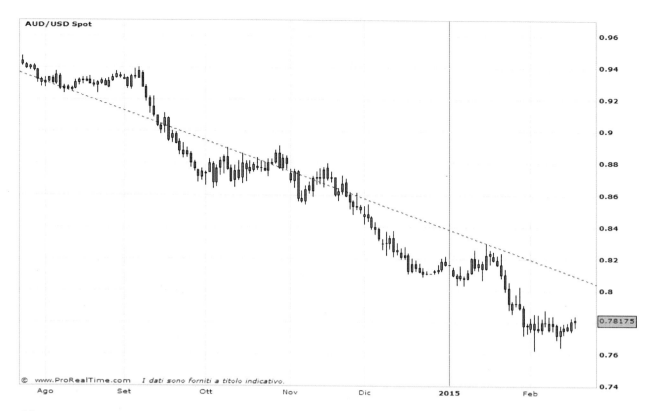

Chart 16

Created with Prorealtime

Chart 17

Created with Prorealtime

"Okay, maybe there is no proof. Maybe the Grail is lost forever. But, Sophie, the only thing that matters is what you believe. History shows us Jesus was an extraordinary man, a human inspiration. That's it. That's all the evidence has ever proved. But... when I was a boy... when I was down in that well Teabing told you about, I thought I was going to die, Sophie. What I did, I prayed. I prayed to Jesus to keep me alive so I could see my parents again, so I could go to school again, so I could play with my dog. Sometimes I wonder if I wasn't alone down there. Why does it have to be human *or* divine? Maybe human *is* divine. Why couldn't Jesus have been a father and still be capable of all those miracles?"

Akiva Goldsman, *for the film The Da Vinci Code (2006) based on The Da Vinci Code (2003) by Dan Brown*

6. Trend following indicators

"Maybe the trend is your friend for a few minutes in Chicago, but for the most part it is rarely a way to get rich" - *Jim Rogers*

The most widely used indicators in trend trading are the moving averages, the MACD and the RSI. The following chapters will examine the indicators mentioned more in details. In particular, this chapter and the next two analyze the moving averages and how they can be exploited to perform in trading. It will also deconstruct a series of false beliefs which are not supported by a performance analysis. In a nutshell, the moving averages are built to filter out the noise from erratic price movements. There are different typologies and, when applied and tested to the real markets and to different cross pairs, their performance differs significantly. The main types of moving averages are the simple, the exponential and the smoothed ones. They differ in the method of calculation. The simple moving averages are calculated giving an equivalent weight to all the prices. The exponential moving averages, on the other hand, confer a greater weight to the recent prices; finally, the smoothed moving averages give a lower weight to the past prices, without removing them from the calculation. In any case, the moving averages are tools used mainly for detecting the direction of a trend, and for finding theoretical points of support and resistance only in part. Although a two hundreds period moving average is generally predicted to act as a support, in case of downtrend, and as resistance, in case of uptrend, there is no practical evidence backing such prediction. In general, a movement does not systematically change direction after coming in contact with a two hundred periods moving average. This theory is not realistic, otherwise no changes of trend were possible. Changes of trend are instead a fundamental part of trading and they occur despite the moving averages.

In addition, what type of moving average should a trader use as supports or as resistances? Simple, exponential or weighted? As specified earlier, there are relevant differences in the method of calculation, so that different types of moving averages provide different levels of support and resistance. The biggest flaw in moving averages lies then in the lack of objectivity. At their discretion, for detecting support and resistance, some traders use a fifty or one hundred periods while others opt for the two hundred periods. It is then appropriate to specify that supports and resistances are only those levels of price that have shown to reject repeated attempts of break. Over the past three decades, several trading companies along with individual traders have developed expert advisors, based on the use of the moving averages. The results are often quite negative and the performances vary widely, based on the type of moving averages used. Besides, a trading system based on the moving averages can perform consistently for a cross pair, while being at the same time unprofitable for a different one. There are no "magic" moving averages that can predict a future movement with accuracy. The moving averages are lagging indicators because they are based on past prices and they are thus unable to forecast a future price movement. Moreover, the moving averages are not able to identify the "highs" and the "lows" as they perform badly over ranging periods. For this reason, the moving averages are predicted to work better with the stock market where the trends are more stable. By their nature, the moving averages perform badly if a pair has a limited fluctuation over the time. Normally, major pairs move just a few percentage points over a week or a month. The next section will show how short and long moving averages perform in the forex market.

Holy Grail rule number 4:

Trend following indicators can help a trader to recognize a trend. However, *none of them can predict a future movement*. Trend following indicators are not the Holy Grail we are looking for.

"The only way I can be safe is to try to find the Grail"

Glenn Cooper, *The Resurrection Maker*

7. Short Term Moving Averages

"The markets are unforgiving and emotional trading always results in losses"- *Alex Elder*

Emotional trading always results in losses. This is a reason why the short-term moving averages may not be the best indicators for recognizing and riding consistent trends. They include erratic movements which are simple noises of the market, usually generated by the activity of the retail traders. The best way to be successful in trading is to understand what the big players are doing. Central banks, investment banks, prime brokers and trusts are the major players of the market. They always operate according to a plan and never for emotional reasons. They are normally involved in operations of carry trade and hedging against the risk of trading. In chapter 2 we already had a glimpse at hedging, and more will be said further in the book. Now, let us explore what carry trade is? It is a trading strategy based on borrowing a currency from a country with low interest rate, and converting it into the currency of another country with higher interest, possibly investing in other assets. *In this sense, the activity of the big speculators can influence the market direction of a currency, while the small traders cannot generate directional movements to any of the pairs.* The main defect of the short-term moving averages is that they are influenced even by small price movements, what the traders call "noise". Since the currencies tend to fluctuate in a tight range and with no direction, short moving averages are predicted to fail inexorably. When a price is squeezed between a support and a resistance, the only way of being profitable is to operate counter-trend. A trader, therefore, relies on short moving averages only when the market is trending.

Chart 18 shows the Fiber on a daily time frame over seven months. It includes three exponential moving averages at five, ten and fifteen periods. The exponential moving averages are preferred to the simple ones because they give more weight to the recent prices, thus resulting in fewer crossovers.

Yet, the example clarifies how a trading system, based on the crossover of three moving averages generates several losing signals. Between March and April, the system has generated two buy longs and one sell short signal that resulted in three losses. This analysis suggests why the short moving averages cannot help a trader to be profitable. The price is oscillating between 1.06 and 1.14. The *Fiber, therefore, is just moving within a range.* During ranging periods, it is never appropriate to use the moving averages, since they can perform consistently only during trends. *Essentially, all kinds of moving average fail inexorably when a price is trading between two levels.*

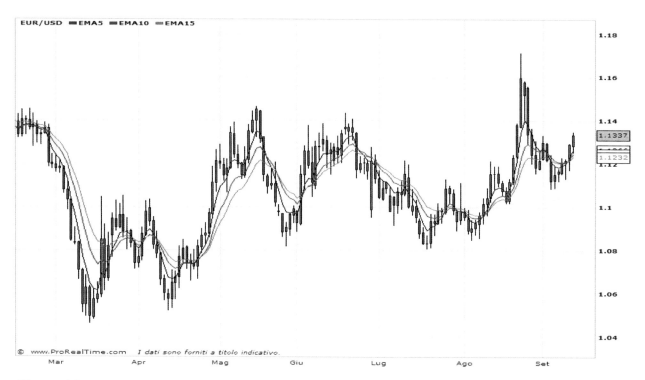

Chart 18

Created with Prorealtime

Chart 19 shows the EUR/USD trend on a four- hour time frame. Since a trend is now recognizable, the use of the exponential moving averages appears to be more proper. Not surprisingly, the trading system generates only two wrong signals. Chart 20 shows how the same trading system fails, when applied to an hourly chart. Over the analyzed period, the Euro is getting stronger against the US Dollar, moving in a stable uptrend. However, since the short moving averages are very close to the price, they react quickly to the natural retracements typical of the uptrends. The outcome is that a trading system based on the crossover of short moving averages does not generate profits, as it results in a series of not profitable "stop and go". In general, short moving averages work better during sharp downtrends rather than during uptrends, since there are fewer retracements.

Chart 21 and 22 show the Fiber trend on a daily time frame. Three simple moving averages at ten, twenty and fifty periods indicate trading signals. Even in this case, however, the crossover of the moving averages generates several wrong signals. As specified, simple moving averages are less reliable than the exponential ones, as the method of calculation assigns the same weight to all of the closing prices. In chart 22 a rectangle highlights the uptrend. Let us see what happened, more in details.

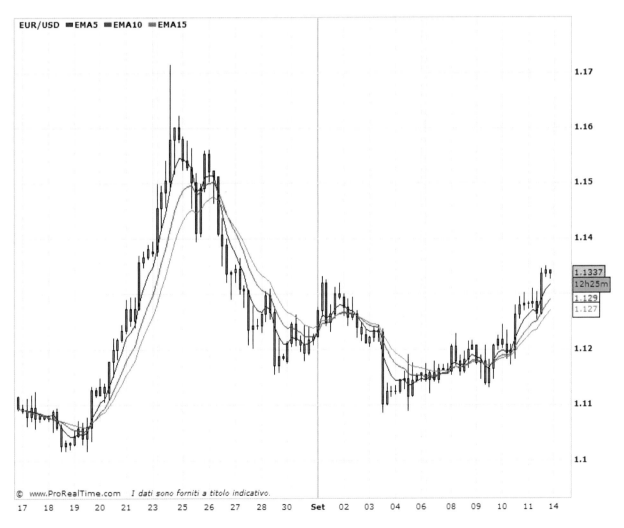

Chart 19

Created with Prorealtime.

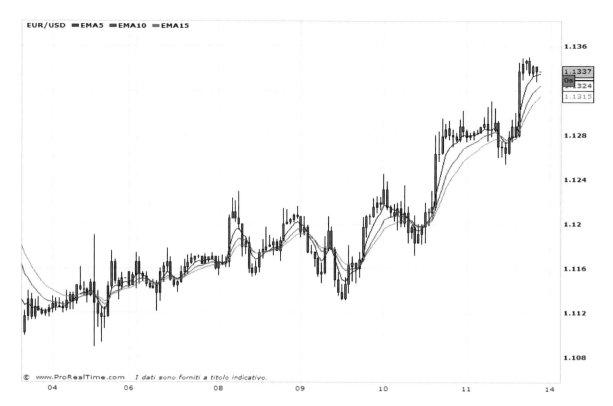

Chart 20

Created with Prorealtime.

Chart 21

Created with Prorealtime

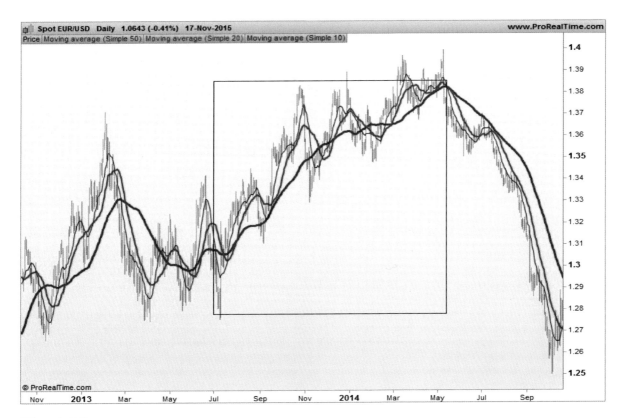

Chart 22

Created with Prorealtime

Since July 2013, the Euro moved upwards against the Greenback, from 1.28 to 1.40, reaching a pick in May 2014. Over the highlighted period, it is possible to identify at least three crossovers that generated wrong trading signals. In conclusion, since the moving averages are lagging indicators, it is often too late to trigger a profitable trade with them.

Holy Grail rule number 5:

Do not fall in love with the idea of trading every single price movement. This is the best way to fail in trading.

"The Templars' mental confusion makes them indecipherable. That's why so many people venerate them."

Umberto Eco, *Foucault's Pendulum*

8. Long Term Moving Averages

"To be a good trader, you need to trade with your eyes open, recognize real trend and turns, and not waste time or energy on regrets and wishful thinking." – *Alexandre Elder*

Traders who use moving averages are aware of the dichotomy between making a moving average as much as possible responsive to the price, and making it not too sensitive in order to avoid entering the position prematurely. In other words, the short-term moving averages are useful to identify changing trends before a large movement occurs, but a system based on these indicators would open and close a position very often because it responds too quickly to changing prices. What might happen is that the price has already experienced a large excursion before the signal is even generated. Long term moving averages allow the traders to avoid trading every single price movement. They are more suitable to recognize consistent trends in comparison to short moving averages, since they filter out the erratic movements. Typical long term moving averages are the one hundred and the two hundred period ones. Taking from the classic technical analysis, however, traders usually evaluate the direction of a trend on the basis of the two hundred periods moving average. In particular, if the price is moving above this line, it follows that the trend is up; conversely, if the price is moving under the two hundred periods moving average, the trend is down. By logic, a trader would then trigger respectively a long and a short trade. This approach, however, is wrong. *The correct way of using the moving averages is to evaluate their linear regression slope:* If the slope is greater than zero, then the trend is moving up; if it is negative, then the trend is moving down. The trick lies on the possibility that the price is moving above the two hundred periods moving average even when the linear regression slope is negative. The classical theory would indicate the possibility to open a long position, whereas the correct interpretation on the use of the moving averages suggests that it is better not to do it. The classic technical analysis often uses a crossover based on a fifty and a two hundred periods moving average. A *golden cross* is generated when the fifty periods moving average crosses above the two hundred periods moving average. A *death cross* is originated in the opposite case. Several studies have demonstrated that trading systems applied to modern forex markets and based on a golden and death cross are not performing consistently over the time. The next two charts illustrate the Fiber trend on a daily chart. The first example shows a fifty and a two hundred periods simple moving averages, while the second example uses the exponential ones. Clearly, the crossover of the moving averages provides no advantage to the trader. For determining the upward nature of the trend, it would be sufficient to see how the price moves in a sequence of higher-highs and higher-lows. Also, as noted above, in April, the linear regression slope of the fifty periods moving average is negative, while the price rose above the moving average. Given the classical technical analysis, a trader could open a long position, which unfortunately would generate a loss. Thus, opening a long trade with a negative slope of the linear regression is never recommendable.

Chart 24 shows the golden cross. As pointed out, the exponential moving averages usually perform better than the simple ones due to a smaller amount of whipsaws. However, in the specific case, there are just minimal improvements of the performance, since the crossover system does not eliminate the false signals occurring between April and July 2014. In fact, the crossover system generated two sell signals that would result in a loss, since the price moves in range, not showing a defined trend. The price began moving in trend only in August. How can a trader evaluate which crossover has the best possibilities to perform consistently? The only way is to back test several trading systems using different typologies of crossovers. However, a back test provides results that are related to the past, for this reason it is not guaranteed that a same trading system will have a similar performance in the future. Furthermore, the same system can perform well with a particular pair and perform poorly with another. Over all, the main flaw of the moving averages is the lack of objectivity, since they do not offer clear reference points.

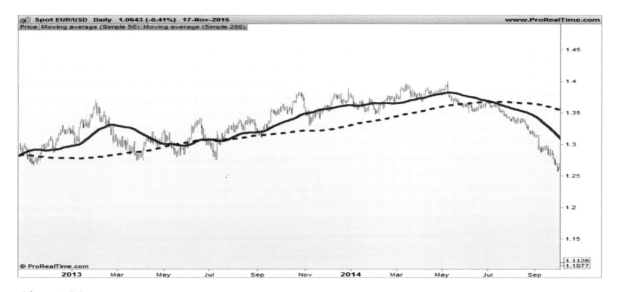

Chart 23

Created with Prorealtime

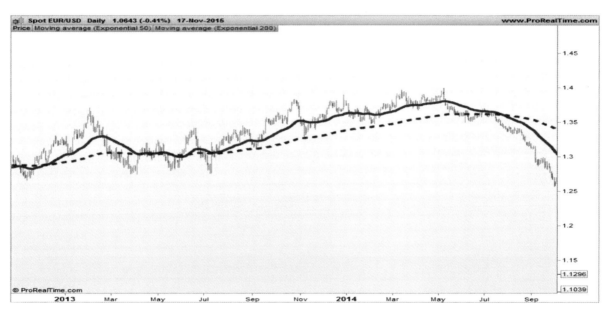

Chart 24

Created with Prorealtime

Holy Grail rule number 6:

Long term moving averages are better filtering out erratic movement than short term. They allow trading only significant price movements. *Do not follow any crossover system.* The correct way to take advantage of the two hundred periods moving average is the evaluation of the linear regression and its slope: *if it is positive, then the main current trend is up. If it is negative, the trend is down.*

"They were nothing more than modern day pagan worshippers. Congregants of a religion built on greed and hedonism. The trading floor served as their shrine; the phones as their Holy Grail; and the clients as the prophets who would entitle them to choose between putting the next down payment on a Lamborghini or a Mercedes"

Soroosh Shahrivar, *The Rise of Shams*

9. Ribbon Moving Averages Indicator

"I think to be in the upper echelon of successful traders requires an innate skill, a gift. It's just like being a great violinist. But to be a competent trader and make money is a skill you can learn"-*Michael Marcus*

Over the last three decades, traders have sought alternatives to moving averages hoping to generate more reliable trading signals. In this sense, the Ribbon Moving Averages and the Guppy Multiple Moving Average indicators are two variants of the classic moving averages. In particular, the Ribbon Moving Average Indicator is a bundle of moving averages with different period lengths, and it is made up of eight different exponential moving averages. The shortest one is called the base length, and by default, is set at 10. The others are based on the increment property, which is also 10. It is then possible to change parameters, and *in any case, the shorter the number of periods selected, the more sensitive the ribbon indicator.* Like the other indicators based on moving averages, it is a trend following tool; so how to use the indicator? Basically, it is a matter of alignments. When all the averages are aligned and they start to become parallel, the trend is strong and the signal is reliable. When they start widening out and separating, it means that the market is probably reaching an extreme level and the trend may be close to its end. Conversely, when the ribbons start to converge on each other, a trend change is already occurring. The best way to take advantage of this indicator is to wait for the ribbon to consolidate and collapse on itself. That may often be the warning about a possible breakout. Chart 25 shows the Fiber trend on a weekly basis, from 2011 to date. The chart includes the Ribbon indicator which correctly detected four main trends, two up, and two down. In July 2011 and 2014, the indicator suggested a short entry and in both cases, and the performance is brilliant. At the end of 2010, the ribbons started to converge on each other, signaling a change of trend. The same happened in November 2012, signaling the beginning of an uptrend. The indicator performed consistently well because of the choice of applying it to a large time frame. Most likely, it would not have performed in such a brilliant way if applied to a much shorter time frame.

Chart 26 shows the Fiber trend on a daily time frame: over the 2014, the Euro depreciated against the US Dollar and the ribbon indicator followed the downtrend, indicating the possible points of change of trend. However, the downtrend was so strong that the ribbons started to converge on each other only in July.

In fact, a trend is over only when all the moving averages converge on each other and the price protrudes from the opposite side.

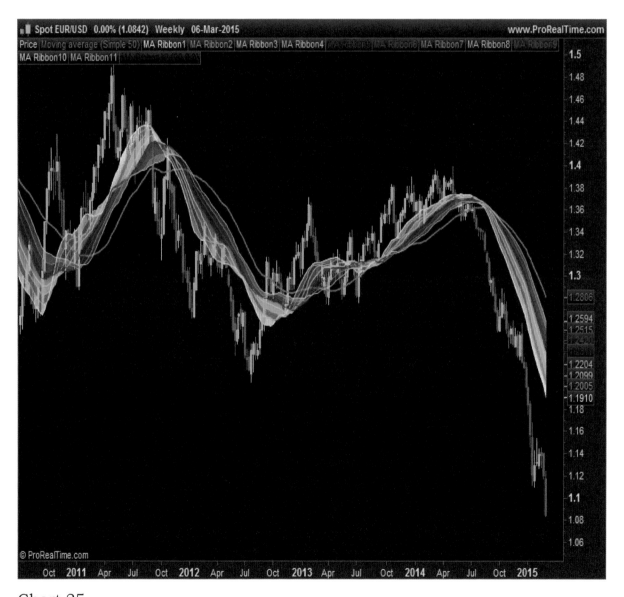

Chart 25

Created with Prorealtime

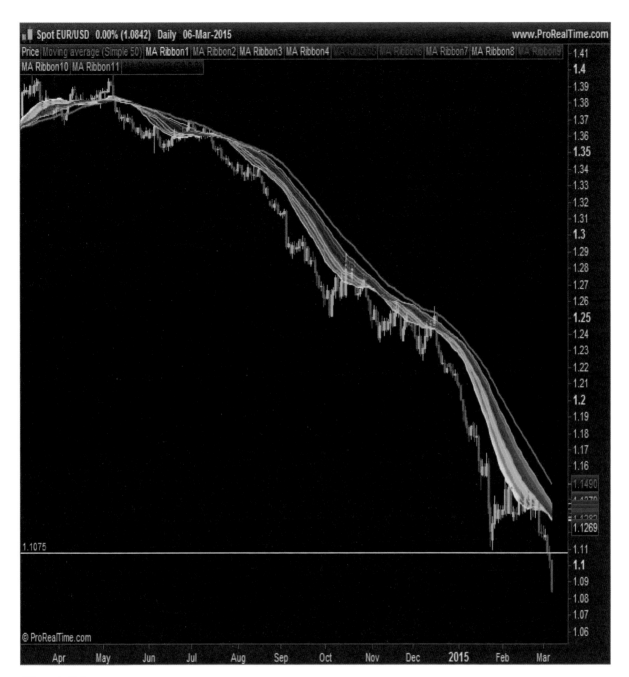

Chart 26

Created with Prorealtime

Holy Grail rule number 7:

The Ribbon moving averages indicator is a valid tool for identifying changing trends.

"The cup, the cup itself, from which our Lord

Drank at the last sad supper with his own....

If a man

Could touch or see it, he was healed at once,

By faith, of all his ills. But then the times

Grew to such evil that the holy cup

Was caught away to Heaven, and disappeared."

The Holy Grail (1842)

10. Guppy Multiple Moving Averages

"I think it was a step forward in my trading education when I realized at last that when old Mr. Partridge kept on telling other customers, "Well, you know this is a bull market!" he really meant to tell them that the big money was not in the individual fluctuations but in the main movement-that is, not in reading the tape but in sizing up the entire market and its trend." – *Jessie Livermore*

The Guppy Multiple Moving Average is an indicator developed by Daryl Guppy. It consists of two groups of moving averages with different time periods. One group is built with short time frame moving averages and one with long term moving averages. In general, if the short-term moving averages are moving above the long-term ones, the trend is bullish. Conversely, when the short-term averages are below the long-term ones, the trend is bearish. When the two groups intersect each other, a trend change is expected.

So, how can a trader benefit from the use of this indicator? The main benefit is certainly the possibility to trade well-established trends, and to recognize those that are changing. Ideally, it would be appropriate to trigger only trades in the same direction as the long term averages. However, when both groups are compressed, the trend is expected to change. In this case, given the uncertainty of the moment, it would be appropriate to wait for the bands to reopen and to generate a new trading signal. In particular, if the group of the short term moving averages resumes the original direction, the new trend is usually quite strong. Furthermore, the indicator can help the trader to evaluate unusual price movements, such as dips and spikes. This happens when the two groups of moving averages diverge too far from each other.

Chart 27 shows the Aussie trend on a daily time frame. The upper section displays the price, while the bottom includes the indicator. In the specific example, the indicator is set with a bundle of fast moving averages from 3 to 15 periods, and a group of six slow moving averages from 30 to 60 periods. Over all, the chart exhibits five main trends. The indicator follows each single trend, suggesting the correct trading signals. Similarly to the Ribbon Moving Average indicator, it performed consistently with a large time frame and to a trending market. The next example, instead, will explain how to use the indicator in the case of no trending markets. The two white rectangles in chart 28 clearly show that when the short and the long moving averages touch, the trend is exhausted. Although the reopening of the bands generally originates a new strong trend, before opening a trade is appropriate to wait until the short and long moving averages diverges completely from each other. Normally, if the price has experienced an explosive movement upward or downward, the market needs to find a new balance before expecting a new break.

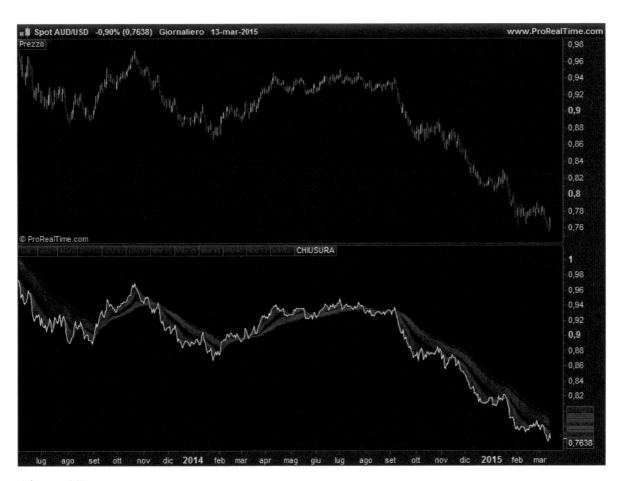

Chart 27

Created with Prorealtime

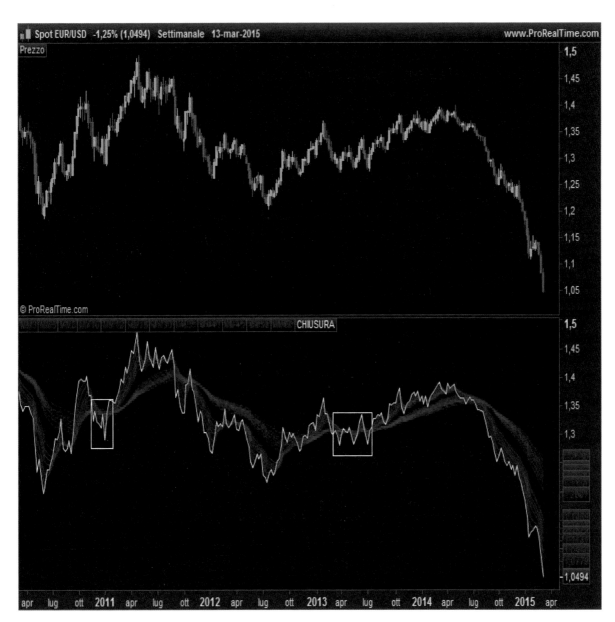

Chart 28

Created with Prorealtime

In other words, if the price moves up strongly, bulls are closing their longs with a profit, while bears are stopped out. In such conditions, a break of the fight should be expected before a new strong movement may occur in a new direction. Chart 29 shows the Euro Dollar trend on a daily basis. Over the selected period, the euro has moved in range, between 1.06 and 1.14. In May, the two groups of moving averages started to intersect each other, suggesting the trader to use only range bound strategies. Without a doubt, in this scenario the recommended course of action for this currency pair is to buy lows and to sell highs.

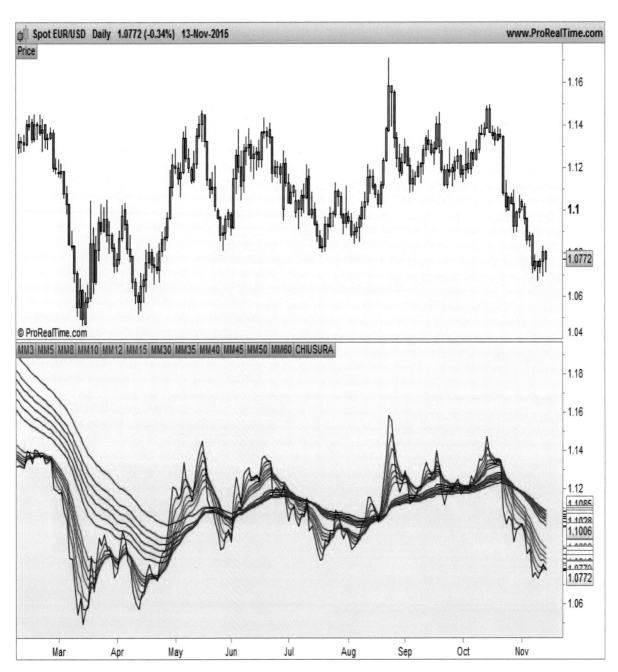

Chart 29

Created with Prorealtime

Holy Grail rule number 8:

Buy Lows and Sell Highs when the two groups of moving averages intersect each other. Trade breakouts when the groups of moving averages diverge each other.

"In 1522 the Templars' Prussian progeny, the Teutonic Knights, secularized themselves, repudiated their allegiance to Rome, and threw their support behind an upstart rebel and heretic named Martin Luther."

Michael Baigent, *Holy Blood, Holy Grail*

11. Macd

"One characteristic I've found among successful traders is that they function effectively when they are not trading. When markets become very quiet and range bound, they occupy themselves with a variety of activities, from sharing ideas with peers to conducting research. Traders who do not tolerate inactivity will inevitably feel the need to trade, often when there is no objective edge present. For them, losing money is less onerous than experiencing boredom". – *In trader Feed*

MACD stands for "Moving Average Convergence/Divergence". Developed by Gerald Appel in the late seventies, it is a trend-following momentum indicator built with two moving averages. It is calculated by subtracting the 12-periods exponential moving average (EMA) from the 26-periods EMA. Closing prices are used for the calculation. The MACD Line oscillates above and below the zero line, known as the centerline. Positive MACD indicates that the upside momentum is increasing. Negative MACD means that the downside momentum is increasing. The "signal line", a nine-period EMA, is used as a trigger for buy and sell signals. The MACD indicator can be used to evaluate the strength of the trend and the turning points of the trend. In general, when the MACD rises, the current trend is bullish. Once the rise stops or levels off, a change of the trend is then possible. The most common way to use the MACD is based on the crossover with its signal line. When the signal line crosses above the MACD, the signal is to sell. When the signal line crosses below the MACD, the signal is to buy. Like the other trend-following indicators, the MACD has its downsides. As a trend following indicator, the trading signals will occur when the trend is already in place. Also, the indicator fails when the currency pair does not show any or enough trend. However, there is another way to use the MACD. In fact, the MACD can indicate divergences. A bearish divergence occurs when the MACD is making new lows while the price is rising. A bullish divergence occurs when the MACD rises while the price is falling. Usually, the divergences are more marked if they occur when both of the moving averages are far from the zero line. Chart 30 shows an example of divergence. Furthermore, it is a necessary to underline the difference between regular and hidden divergences. If the *price* is making new higher highs or lower lows and the oscillator does not follow suit, then a reversal is expected. This is a classic divergence. Hidden divergences, instead, occurs when the *oscillator* is making new higher highs or lower lows, and the price does not follow suit. The main difference is that in this case the expected reversal against the trend is small. This may give to the trader the opportunity to enter on a pullback of the current trend. In other words, the trader can have the possibility to trade a consolidate trend, which is less risky than trading a reverse.

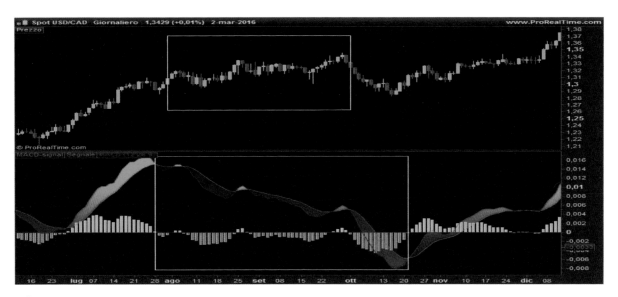

Chart 30

Created with Metatrader 5.0

Regular Divergence:

- Higher highs in the price and lower highs in the oscillator. A trend reversal is expected from up to down.

- Lower lows in the price and higher lows in the oscillator. A trend reversal from down to up is expected.

Hidden Divergence:

- Lower highs in the price and higher highs in the oscillator. A confirmation of the price trend which is down is expected.

- Higher lows in the price and lower lows in the oscillator. A confirmation of the price trend which is up is expected.

Chart 31 shows the Fiber trend on a daily time frame. Over six months, the Euro moved from 1.06 to 1.1150, testing several times the support at 1.06 and the resistance at 1.14. For the analysis, it will be assumed that short or long signals are triggered when the signal line crosses above or under the MACD. From March onwards, the indicator generated four buy and four sell signals. Back- testing the trading system, the outcome is negative. The reason is that the price is moving in a range. Chart 32 shows how the Euro performed against the Canadian Dollar on a weekly timeframe. Over the 2013, the Euro gained against the Canadian Dollar, moving in a stable uptrend. In June 2013, the MACD crosses above its signal line, thus riding a consistent trend until its end in March 2014. The histogram was above the zero giving a confirmation about the strength of the trend. In March 2014, the MACD line crosses under its signal, signaling the beginning of a downtrend. As mentioned, the trader can analyze even the momentum. The histogram followed the downtrend, reaching its deepest point in July 2014. While the price fell even more, the histogram started to converge towards the zero, warning about a possible trend reversal.

Chart 31

Created with Prorealtime

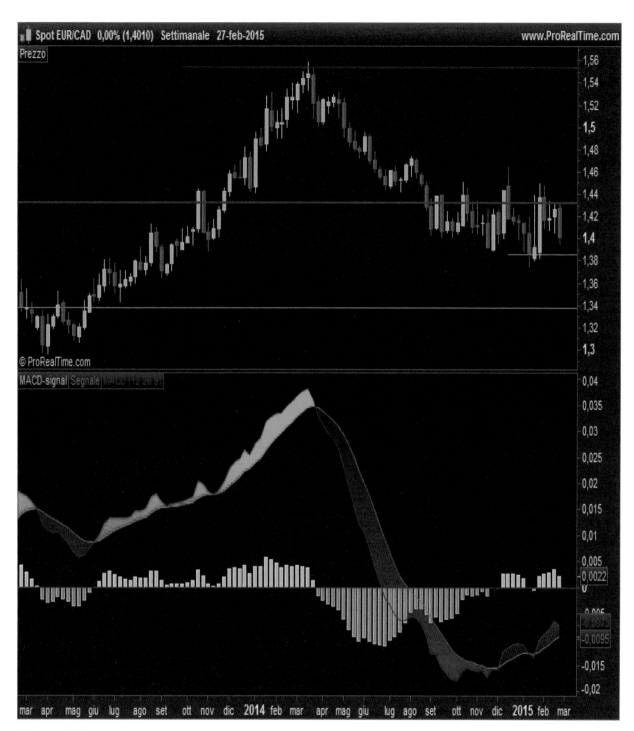

Chart 32

Created with Prorealtime

Holy Grail rule number 9:

Do not use the MACD crossover to enter a trade. *Use it, instead, to forecast a future price movement if a regular or a hidden divergence is detected.*

"All members of the order were obliged to wear white habits of surcoats and cloaks, and these soon evolved into the distinctive white mantle for which the Templars became famous."

Michael Baigent, *Holy Blood, Holy Grail*

12. Relative Strength Index (RSI)

"I believe the very best money is made at the market turns. Everyone says you get killed trying to pick tops and bottoms and you make all your money by playing the trend in the middle. Well for twelve years I have been missing the meat in the middle but I have made a lot of money at tops and bottoms."- *Paul Tudor Jones*

Developed by J. Wilder, The Relative Strength Index (RSI) is a momentum oscillator and is used to measure the magnitude of a movement. By default, the indicator is set at 14-periods with two thresholds marked at 70 and 30, or at more extreme values, such as 80 and 20. The use of the RSI is often misinterpreted; when traders analyze the indicator, they tend to look at overbought or oversold thresholds. Some open short trades immediately after the indicator oscillates around the +70 thresholds or they trigger long trades when the indicator moves into the 30 threshold. However, during strong and extended trends, the indicator can oscillate around the overbought or the oversold area for long periods of time. Unfortunately, this very important distinction on the use of RSI is rarely mentioned in the trading manuals. Many authors merely point out that the RSI can move within overbought or oversold for a long time, but they are unable to explain when it is appropriate to follow the trend or when to open counter - trend trades. In this analysis a general rule is that, *if the price is forming a series of higher-highs and higher-lows, the trader should look for an overbought RSI and enter a long trade. Conversely, if the price is forming a series of lower-highs and lower-lows the trader is looking for an oversold RSI to place a short trade. When, on the other hand the price is moving between two well defined areas of resistance and support, the trader should look at the overbought area and open a short trade, or a long trade once the indicator moves into oversold.* The RSI has also a center line at a reading of 50. If the RSI is moving above 50, the momentum is considered up, while a drop below 50 would indicate that the momentum is down. Like in the case of the other technical indicators, the RSI is more effective when used on longer time-frames.

Chart 33 shows the Fiber on one-hour time-frame. The example highlights how placing a short trade when the indicator moves into overbought area might be risky. Between the 19th and the 20th, a long white candle appeared and the RSI moved into overbought. As a general rule, before opening any trade, it is always appropriate to wait and see if the price breaks the resistance. In case below, the price has broken the resistance, above 1.12. Simply put, there was no retracement of the price, although the indicator moved into overbought. Now, a trader should only look for long trades.

Chart 33

Created with Prorealtime

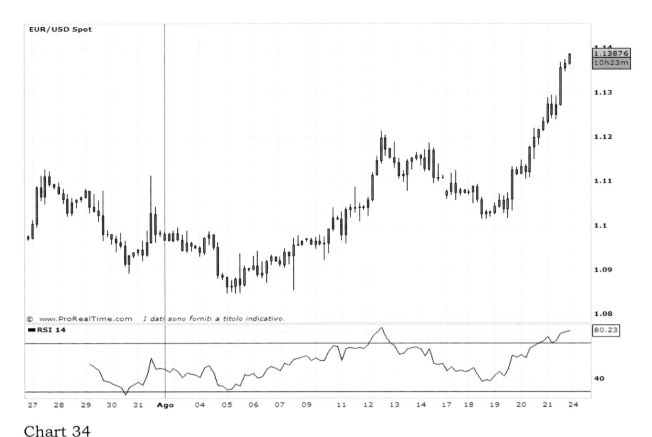

Chart 34

Created with Prorealtime

Chart 34 shows the Euro/Dollar trend on a four-hour time-frame. The indicator has identified two oversold and two overbought areas, so let us examine how the price reacted. Between the end of July and the beginning of August, the RSI was oversold. The price trend changed and, in particular, on August 5, the bears failed to break the support. On August 12, the RSI moved into overbought with the price hitting new highs, moving from 1.105 to 1.12. It was, however, a fake break, as immediately after, the price moved back to 1.10. Only on August 20, the bulls were finally able to break the resistance, pushing the price higher to hit new highs. How is it then possible to determine whether the trend will continue or reverse? Once the RSI moves into an overbought or an oversold area, it is appropriate to wait and to see where and how the price is going to move. If the price moves within a well-defined range and the indicator moves back from the overbought or the oversold area, it may be an opportunity to open a counter–trend trade. On the other hand, if the price moves in a strong trend, it may be an opportunity to open a trade on the same direction of the main trend.

Chart 35
Created with Prorealtime

Chart 35 shows the Fiber on a daily time frame. Over the analyzed period, the pair moved in a range between 1.05/1.06 and 1.14. In the lower section it is displayed the RSI. Between March and April, the indicator moved into oversold after the price tumbled from 1.14 to approximately 1.05. Bulls were then able to push the price higher to the previous threshold at 1.14. Between May and June, the indicator made a triple top, with the price unable to break the resistance at 1.14. The latter is the new resistance level, while 1.06 and 1.08 are the supports. A trader is now aware that the pair is moving in a range. Based on the rule explained in this chapter, it may be best to apply only a range strategy. As specified, a trader should never be afraid to trade ranging charts, since several statistics estimate that the market moves in range or in an erratic way 70% of the time. Only if the price breaks above 1.16, the trader is then looking forward to trade the trend, once a series of higher-highs and higher-lows is formed. In terms of risk prevention, if the price breaks the resistance, the stop loss should be positioned under the previous low at 1.08. In the case when the price reverses after hitting the resistance at 1.14, a stop loss should be positioned above 1.16. Moreover, the brokers are able to check where the stop losses are and they might be able to hit them. For this reason, it is suggestable either to use a larger stop loss, increasing then the risk, or to hedge trading a high correlate pair. Managing the risk involved in trading, however, will be argument of study in the money management section.

Holy Grail rule number 10:

Traders should open a counter-trend trade if the price moves within a range and if the RSI reverses from the overbought or the oversold threshold. Conversely, if the price moves in a stable trend, traders should open a long or a short trade once the RSI is respectively overbought or oversold.

"The novice swears to keep the secrets of the Order and to

"faithfully defend and maintain the holy Christian faith.. under no less penalty than loss of life, by having my head struck off and placed on the point of a pinnacle or spire, my skull sawn asunder, and my brains exposed to the scorching rays of the sun, as a warning to all infidels and traitors. So help me Christ"

Martin Short, Inside the brotherhood

13. Commodity Channel Index

"Rule number one: Most things will prove to be cyclical. Rule number two: Some of the greatest opportunities for gain and loss come when other people forget rule number one"- *Howard Marks*

Developed by Donald Lambert, the Commodity Channel Index is a momentum oscillator that measures the difference between a price change and its average. Originally created only for the commodities market, it is now widely used even in Forex. The indicator oscillates between two thresholds marked at: + - 100. Like the RSI, the CCI is used to identify the overbought and the oversold price areas or to detect possible trend reversals. The indicator moves into overbought when it surges above +100 and into oversold when it falls under -100. If the price is moving in a strong trend, a trader can open a long trade once the indicator moves into overbought; if, conversely, the CCI moves into oversold a trader can trigger a short trade. If the price is moving within a range and the CCI moves into overbought, a trader can open a short trade, while when the indicator moves into oversold, a trader can trigger a long position. A second way to use the CCI is to trade when the indicator crosses over the "zero" line. More specifically, if the indicator moves back from the overbought area and it crosses over the zero line, a trader should only look for short trades, whereas in the opposite case a trader should be looking for long trades. Like the RSI, even the CCI can be used to detect a divergence, providing a warning about a potential reversal, since the momentum is not confirming the price action. A bullish divergence is formed when the price makes a lower low, while the indicator makes a higher low, indicating a smaller down-ward momentum. A bearish divergence occurs when the price hits a higher high while the CCI hits a lower high, which indicates a smaller upside momentum. A trader should always be aware that divergences can be misleading in a strong trend. In fact, when the price is moving in one direction strongly, it is possible to see several bearish divergences before the price hits a high. The indicator can be also used to identify price cycles. A cycle can be defined as a repetition of a movement on a regular basis. Cycles are not only object of financial study, since cyclical phenomena normally occur in nature (such as the phases of the moon, or more marked turning of the seasons above and below certain latitudes). Let us see what characterizes a cycle. Firstly, lows are normally used to define a cycle's length and to forecast future cycle lows. However, it might happen that a low may not appear in strong uptrends. Similarly, a high may not be seen during strong declines. Secondly, the cycles are often not identical since, they differ in amplitude and length, and can even disappear at times. Thirdly, during bull markets, prices peak in the latter part of the cycle. Conversely, during bear markets, prices usually peak in the front half of the cycle. The cycle analysis is used by traders to identify turning points. Simply put, traders should analyze trends to establish direction and cycles to anticipate turning points.

Chart 36
Created with Prorealtime

Chart 36 shows the Fiber, on 1hr time-frame. For this analysis, we can use the same chart used to explain how the RSI works. The choice is not casual. The purpose is to study whether the two indicators provide similar trading information. However, the CCI generates a larger number of whipsaws than RSI. In other words, it oscillates more than the RSI. On the 19th a long white candle is a signal that bulls are trying to push the quotation higher. With the CCI bullish signal in force along with the white Marubozu, focus will be only on bullish setups. Even on the 14th, the indicator generated a bullish signal, which it should not be followed since the volatility is compressed and there is no a long white candle which might think about a breakout. With regards to the study of cycles, it is not possible to accurately identify the duration, since the hourly chart displays a price that moves erratically from 14th to 19th. Therefore, in order to evaluate the price cycle, it is appropriate to analyze larger time-frame charts.

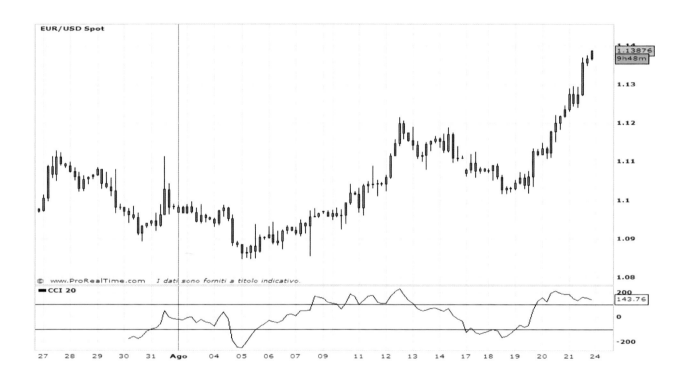

Chart 37

Created with Prorealtime

Chart 37 shows the price trend on 4h time-frame chart. In this example, the indicator shows more accurate signals than the ones shown on 1hr chart. In particular, between July 30th and August 5th, two lows are observed. The first low should be then evaluated as a false end-point of the descending cycle, because the cycle actually ends on August 5th. From this date onwards, a new cycle starts, with a high on August 13th and with the cycle ending between the 18th and 19th of August when the indicator reaches a new low. Again, from this point on, a new cycle is formed, with a new high in conjunction with the break-up of the previous one. The daily chart shows cycles of about a month and a half. In particular, chart 38 shows five cycles. In every cases the indicator hits a low roughly every month and a half. Only the last cycle, the one formed between late May and mid-July, has a slightly greater length. The last cycle hits a double bottom with the price quoting first at 1.10 and then at 1.08. This can create some trouble to a trader, since it is difficult to predict a low with accuracy. The monthly chart (shown in chart 39) perfectly illustrates alternating cycles. The first cyclical price low is identified in mid-2010, while between 2012 and 2013 the indicator suggests the beginning of a second cycle. At the beginning of 2015, the indicator identifies a new low which can be considered to be the beginning of a third cycle. As a matter of fact, in 2015 the indicator moved back from the oversold threshold, thus suggesting a possible rise of the Euro against the US Dollar.

Chart 38

Created with Prorealtime

Chart 39

Created with Prorealtime

The analysis of the cycles of the last six years thus suggests that a cycle is formed every 2 years. The cycles are not exactly the same; in fact, the last cycle lasted longer than the previous. A better indication on the analysis of cycles could be obtained using data from the past 15 years. In this way the presence and the average duration of cycles is more easily discernable.

Holy Grail rule number 11:

The CCI can help a trader to better visualize price cycles. They are detectable for any time frame, but they are more evident on larger timeframes. *A new cycle is detected when the CCI reaches a low and once it crosses back from the oversold threshold.*

"The sweet vision of the Holy Grail drove me from all vainglories, rivalries, and earthly heats that spring and sparkle out... "

Alfred, Lord Tennyson

14. Candlestick trading and price patterns

"Your ultimate success or failure will depend on your ability to ignore the worries of the world long enough to allow your investments to succeed."-

Peter Lynch

Candlesticks trading

None of the analyzed indicator can guarantee the trader to be profitable over time. The reason is that all of them are discretionary; in other words, they lack objectivity. Yet, many authors and brokers advertise different trading systems based on such indicators claiming that they are almost infallible and forecasting successful operations to the naïve and unexperienced traders. This lack of ethics does not lead to learn what really works in trading, but only to sales of books and software. Without a doubt, a trader needs additional tools to trade with greater objectivity. For this reason, it is time to see how a trader can benefit from the study of the different typologies of Japanese candlesticks and price patterns. The Japanese candlesticks are real time indicators of the markets' emotions, (fear and greed). The Japanese used the candlesticks to trade rice in the 17th century and much of development is credited to a legendary rice trader named Homma. The candlestick trading is based on the assumption that all of the known information is reflected in the price and that buyers and sellers trade on expectations and emotions. The candlesticks are composed of two parts: the body and the shadow. By definition, when the "close" is higher than the "open", the candlestick is bullish, while, on the opposite case, the candlestick is bearish. The "high" is the maximum price and the "low" is the minimum price during the formation of the candlesticks.

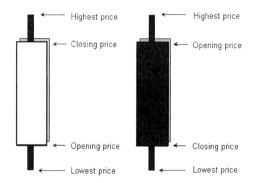

Here follow the most effective types of candlesticks and price patterns.

1.   <u>Marubozu candlesticks</u>

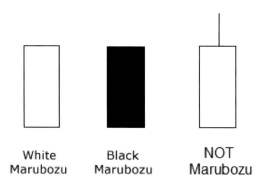

White   Black   NOT
Marubozu   Marubozu   Marubozu

Marubozu are no shadow candlesticks. A Bullish Marubozu is a candlestick with same "close" and "high", while the "open" is the same as the "low". Bullish Marubozu indicates that the bulls have the control. *The longer the candlesticks, the stronger the bulls.* A Bearish Marubozu is a candlestick which has a "close" the same as the "low" and the "open" is the same as the "high". A Bearish Marubozu indicates that the bears have the control. *The longer the candlestick, the stronger the bears.*

A bullish Marubozu might be seen at the beginning of an uptrend. Traders could then trigger a buy when the following candlestick breaks above the bullish Marubozu and a series of higher-highs and higher-lows is in place. Similarly, at the beginning of a downtrend if a bearish Marubozu appears, traders could trigger a short when the following candlestick breaks below the previous bearish Marubozu. If a bearish Marubozu appears during a strong uptrend, it is suggested to wait before opening a short trade. In fact, a single bearish Marubozu can be just the result of a take profit. If a trader holds a long position and a very long bearish Marubozu appears, the trade should be closed, taking profit. On the opposite case, the trader should take profit, when during a short trade, a very long bullish Marubozu appears at the end of a downtrend.

2.   Doji

A Doji is a candlestick with the same "open" and "close". These candlesticks have neither body nor color, since bulls and bears are balanced and they are signals of indecision and uncertainty. How to trade a Doji? In trading with a Doji, whether holding a profitable position or willing to open a new trade, it is always better to wait and to see what the next price direction might be. There are different types of Doji candlesticks.

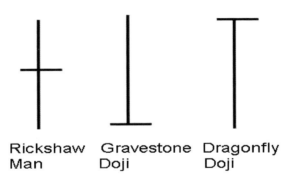

Rickshaw Man   Gravestone Doji   Dragonfly Doji

The **Rickshaw Man** is a strong signal of indecision. It can appear at the end of an uptrend, or in the middle or at the end of a downtrend.

The **Gravestone Doji** appears at the top of an uptrend. It is usually a warning signal and it is appropriate to wait for the next candlesticks as a reversal is possible.

The **Inverted Gravestone** or **Dragonfly** is a Doji candlestick that can appear at the bottom of the market.

3.   Hammer and Hanging Man

The Hammer is a kind of candlestick that can appear at the bottom of a downtrend. The Hammer has a small to not existent upper shadow. The Hanging Man, instead, is usually seen at the top of an uptrend.

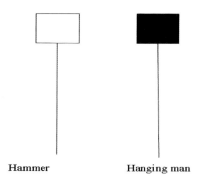

Hammer   Hanging man

Hammer and Hanging Man have three identifying features:

1. The body is in the upper third of the price range.

2. The lower shadow is twice of the length of the body at least.

3. They have no or a very short upper shadow.

Hammer and Hanging man indicate a possible reversal.

4.   <u>**Shooting Star**</u>

The Shooting Star typically appears at the top of an uptrend. It indicates that bulls have failed to push the price higher, and that the bears were able to reject it back.

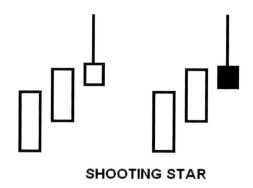

SHOOTING STAR

In general, the candlesticks are extremely useful, especially when combined with other ones, to form the so called "price patterns", which are examined in more details below.

5.   Engulfing Pattern

The Engulfing Pattern is a high probability reversal signal. The Engulfing Pattern consists of two candlesticks with different colors. The body of the second candlestick completely engulfs the body of the first one. The Engulfing pattern is even more effective when the second candlestick has a long body and it can engulf more than one candlestick.

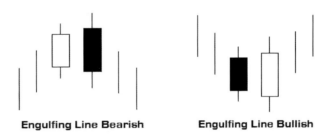

Engulfing Line Bearish   **Engulfing Line Bullish**

6.   Dark Cloud Cover

It is another bearish reversal price pattern that is usually found at the top of an uptrend. It is made of two candlesticks. It originates when the second candlestick opens above the high of the first candlestick, and it closes below the mid-point between the open and the close of the previous day.

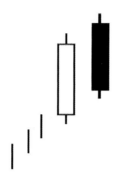

7. Piercing Line

The Piercing Line is the opposite of the Dark Cloud Cover. In this case, the second candlestick opens below the low of the first one and it closes between the open and the close of the previous candlestick. The meaning of this pattern is that the bearish forces tried to push lower the price, with a break below the low of the first candle. However, the bulls were able to push back the price above the low of the first candle.

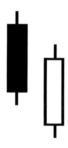

8. Harami

A sequence of two candlesticks can also forms an Harami Pattern. The bigger candlestick engulfs the whole body of the smaller one. *The bigger the difference between the length of two candlesticks is, the more effective the signal.* In some cases, a Harami pattern may represent a reversal signal, but it should always be confirmed by the next candlesticks, since it is not as reliable as the dark cloud cover or the piercing line.

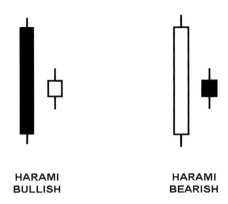

9. <u>Morning and Evening Star</u>

The Morning Star pattern is constituted by three candlesticks. This pattern occurs at the bottom of a downtrend and it is a high probability signal of reversal. The first candlestick is a bearish one. The second candlestick is much smaller than the first one and it is positioned below the first one. It can be bearish or bullish. The third candlestick is a bullish one and it is positioned above the second one, covering a large portion of the first candlestick. The evening star pattern is exactly the opposite of the morning star and it is normally found at the end of an uptrend.

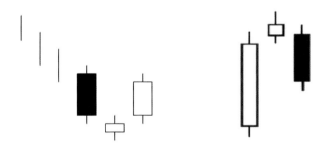

10. Geometric Patterns

The following price patterns are derived by the geometric analysis. In particular, the most commonly patterns are shown. Flags, pennants, ascending, descending and symmetrical triangles are important tools which cannot be ignored by any trader and they usually generate a very good chance

78

of profitability. The graphical representation from below allows the trader to understand how to trade. It is important that the trader follows the break of the price, placing a trade in favor of the trend.

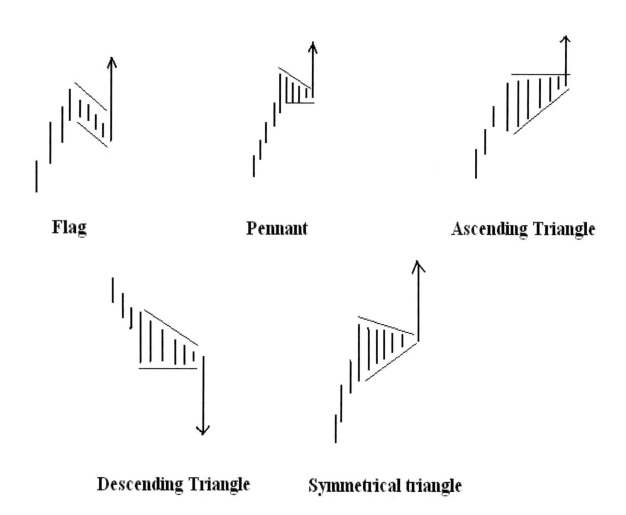

Flag   Pennant   Ascending Triangle

Descending Triangle   Symmetrical triangle

The example from below shows two symmetrical triangles. It shows how the Greenback moved against the Canadian dollar on a weekly basis. Over 2013, the Us Dollar got stronger, moving from 0.96 to 1.10. Once the price breaks up the resistance of the first triangle, it is visible a strong movement upward from 1.16 to 1.28 in almost a vertical way. A second triangle is then formed, and the break at 1.26 is such a strong one to push the price until 1.46. A trader should always trade the price action and learn to identify the geometric patterns shown above. Hereafter, are shown three examples of price action.

11. Parabolic Curve

The Parabolic Curve is an outstanding price pattern. A parabolic curve is formed when the price regression line is moving in an exponential way. These moves normally occur during periods of huge speculation, normally associated to a formation of a bubble. What happens is that speculators are able to push the price strongly higher. Trader can follow the trend at the beginning of trend, being careful to take profit before a reverse.

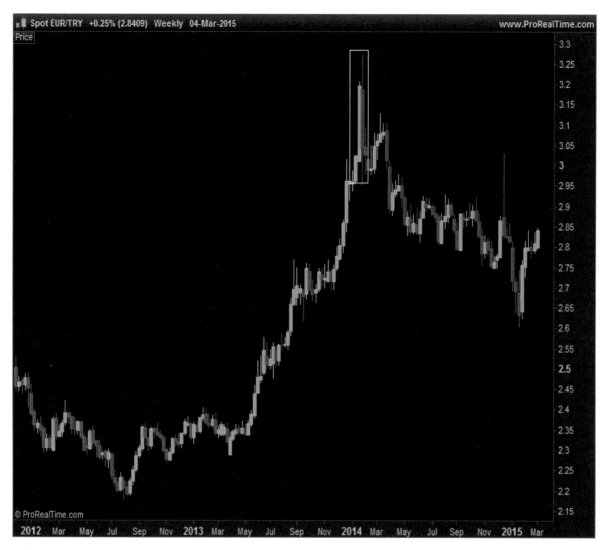

Chart 40

Chart 40
Created with Prorealtime

Chart 40 shows how the Euro moved against the Turkish Lira on a weekly basis. It is a nice example of a parabolic curve. Since August 2012, the pair moved in a strong uptrend, in a smooth sequence of higher–highs and higher-lows. Notably, between the end of 2013 and the beginning of 2014, the price linear regression became almost vertical in association with candlesticks of increased amplitude. When the linear regression assumes such an angle, what happens is that the big players are taking profits, while retail traders are entering in the market late, only to be then stopped out. It is thus recommended to never get long positions when the linear regression is almost vertical. It is normally too late for being profitable. In fact, at the beginning of the 2014, a bearish candlestick with a long tail fully engulfs the previous long white candle, indicating that the uptrend is over.

Chart 41

Created with Prorealtime

Chart 41 shows the Euro/Dollar trend on a monthly time-frame. Two engulfing bearish patterns and one bullish Morningstar are highlighted within rectangles. A first engulfing bearish pattern is visible at the end of 2009 and a second one is visible at the beginning of 2013. In both cases, the price fell down. In the first case, the pair tumbled from 1.50 to 1.20 in five months, while in the second case, initially the price did not drop and rather there was an attempt to break above the resistance, but then the price fell violently until 1.08. In May 2010, in May 2010, a bullish Morningstar in area 1.20 perfectly highlighted the rise of the price back up to 1.50.

Chart 42 shows how the US Dollar moved against the Swiss Franc on a weekly time frame. Over the end of 2011 and for more than half of 2012, the Us Dollar depreciated against the Franc, falling from the parity until 0.70. The downtrend was strong until August, when bulls were finally able to reverse the trend. The rectangle highlights an outstanding hammer with a very long tail. No other comments are needed.

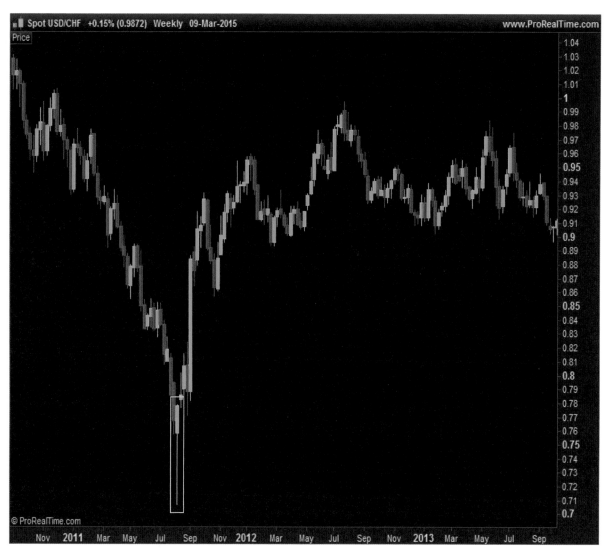

Chart 42

Source: Prorealtime

Holy Grail rule number 12:

The principle of physics and geometry are valid also when applied to the financial markets. A trader should then look for horizontal and oblique resistances and supports, ascending and descending triangles, parabolic curve and so on. *Price patterns are more effective than indicators to forecast a future movement.* The reason is simple: while the indicators are derivative from the price, *candlesticks and price patterns represent a real time snapshot of what is happening in the market.*

"The gods know what's important, what's wrong about you. They know everything. If you go out searching for the Holy Grail, they won't let you find it."

Tom Spanbauer, *In the City of Shy Hunters*

15. Price Action – Breakouts and volatility

"Volatility is greatest at turning points, diminishing as a new trend becomes established"-George Soros

Volatility is a rate at which the price of a cross pair increases or decreases for a given set of returns. By definition, volatility is high when a large price movement occurs within a short amount of time. Conversely, volatility is low when a little movement occurs in a short period of time. So, how can volatility be exploited? Ideally, a trader should trade those pairs that are moving next to some relevant resistance or support level.

If the price is trading near a threshold and it is testing it several times, it may be a sign that a breakout is next to occur soon. A trader should then be ready to trade on the same direction of the breakout once it occurs and the volatility skyrockets. There are two main ways to measure the volatility: the Bollinger Bands or the Average True Range (ATR). The ATR measures the average trading range of the market for X amount of time. For instance, if the ATR is set to 20 on a daily chart, it shows the average trading range for the past twenty days. When the ATR is falling, the volatility is decreasing. When the ATR is rising, the volatility is increasing. Breakouts and volatility work in association. A volatility increase is necessary to generate a breakout. Fake breakouts in general occur when volatility is not strongly increasing. Let's now see a few examples of breakouts.

Chart 43 shows the Us Dollar versus the Swiss Franc on a daily time frame. For the first half of 2014, the pair moved between 0.875 and 0.915. In September, a white Marubozu candle breaks above the 0.9150 threshold. Breakout is strong enough to push the price higher until the parity at the end of 2014. Horizontal breakouts are excellent patterns for making profits. However, not all of the breakouts are valid to trigger a trade, since resistances and supports are fighting levels for bulls and bears.

Chart 43

Created with Metatrader 5.0

How is then possible to avoid fake signals? The Following signs may help to recognize a valid breakout.

1. The price has previously tested the resistance or the support levels several times, but in association with a low volatility.

2. A long white or a black candle breaks the resistance or the support.

3. A strong increase in volatility.

4. A second or a third candle breaks the high or the low of the first one.

A long trade is then triggered once the next candle breaks above the high of the one which broke the resistance. Shorts are triggered on the next candle which is closing below the low of the one which broke the support. It is then recommended to not take in profits, until the price hits a resistance or a support, recognizable by analyzing a larger timeframe. Ideally, when trading a breakout on a daily chart, it is appropriate to close it, once the price hits a resistance or a support threshold, detectable on a weekly chart. Some traders, on the other hand, prefer closing trades using Fibonacci extensions.

Chart 44 shows a different example of a horizontal breakout on a DKK/NOK cross. A horizontal white line underlines the resistance at 1.14. Over the whole 2013, the Danish Koruna got stronger, generating an uptrend that found a relevant resistance at 1.14. This threshold was tested five times throughout 2014. In November, the bullish forces were finally able to overcome the resistance of the bears, originating an outstanding and almost vertical movement upward, which delivered a sensational profit in just a month. While there are no magic indicators, *price action works!*

Chart 45 shows how the Euro moved against the Norwegian Krone on a weekly timeframe. In 2014, the price has tested several times the resistance at 8.5. Finally, in November, bulls were able to push the price higher. The box highlights the long white candle that breaks the resistance at 8.50. Once it broke this resistance, the Euro gained about 16 % against the Norwegian Krone in a few days. The breakout generated an explosive movement associated with an increase in volatility. Worth noting, is the very long bearish pin ball, which indicates that the bulls have exhausted their driving force and that the bearish forces are now in control of the market, as they are able to reject the price back to the former resistance - now a support - at 8.50. Traders should always know how to trade high volatility movements, because they provide an excellent opportunity to make profits. However, statistics suggest that the retail traders are usually not profitable during the most volatile time of the day. This happens because traders do not know what kind of strategy can be the most profitable based on the time of the day. A relevant difference between the retail and the professional traders is that the latter usually filter trades, applying different strategies at different time of the day.

In other words, applying a breakout strategy to a non- volatile market time is not profitable, while a range-trading strategy does not perform during the most volatile times.

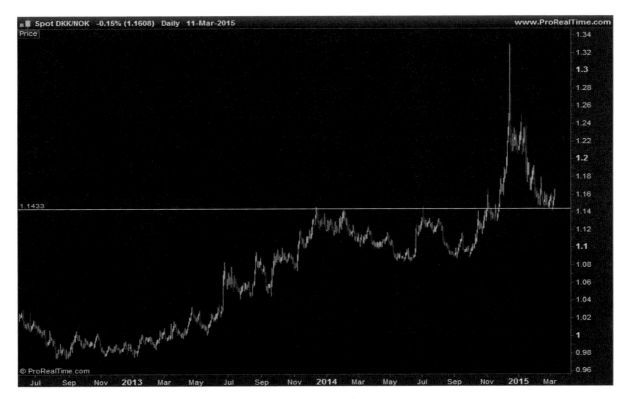

Chart 44

Created with Prorealtime

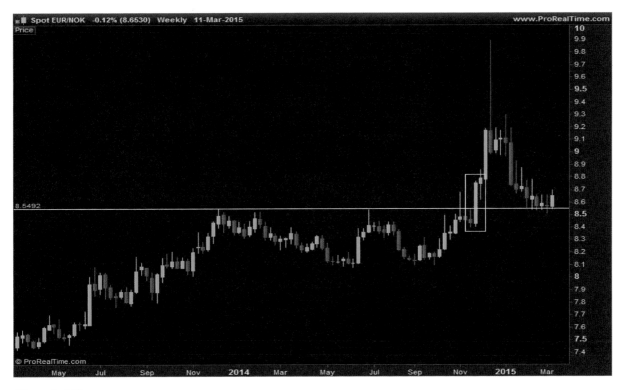

Chart 45

Created with Prorealtime

Forex trading is highly affected by which markets are open. For instance, the EUR/USD is the most liquid cross and its volatility reaches the pick when both New York and London are open. The same concept applies for the GBP/USD and USD/CHF. The USD/JPY is volatile at the start of the Tokyo and New York sessions, while the Aussie and Kiwi volatility increases when Tokyo overlaps Sydney.

The following tables illustrate the dynamics that exist among several markets:

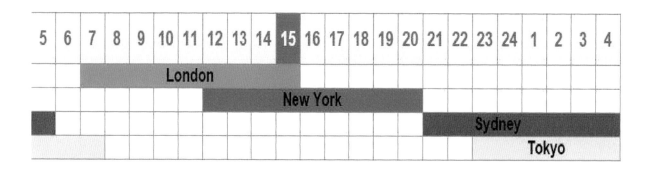

Table 1 Forex Market Hours GMT

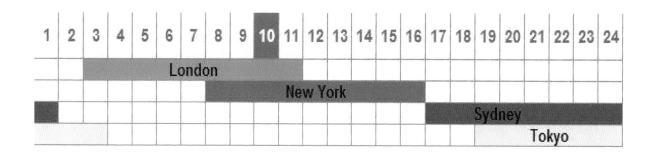

Table 2 Forex Market Hours EST (New York)

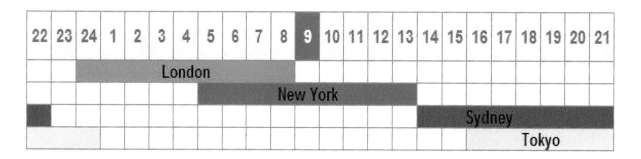

Table 3 Forex Market Hours PST (Los Angeles, Vancouver)

Forex brokers can run several studies, analyzing the data of their clients' accounts. Traders can exploit the results and figure out the best strategy to apply at a certain moment of the day. A research conducted by a main broker has shown how the retails traders, trading the Cable from 4 to 5 am, New York time, generated a profit around 47 % of the time. However, this percentage rose to 55 % of time, when trading from 8 to 9 pm. This outcome is quite impressive. Essentially, there is an intraday seasonality which has an effective impact on trading performance. The Cable volatility, for example, varies widely during the day time. Over the last two years, this cross has moved about 15 to 20 pips per hour, from 2 to 10 am, while only 5 pips from 4 to 11 pm. The same research suggests that there is a negative relationship between the profitability of the retail traders and the volatility. Statistically, the retail traders are more profitable during the Asian trading session, when the volatility is low and the range strategies work the best. The following charts show how the volatility changes during the day. Notably, over the analyzed period, the EUR/USD volatility peaks up from 12am to 15am GMT, while it gets lower after that. In particular, the chart below shows how the Fiber moved from 30 to 40 pips per hour, between 12 am and to 2 pm.

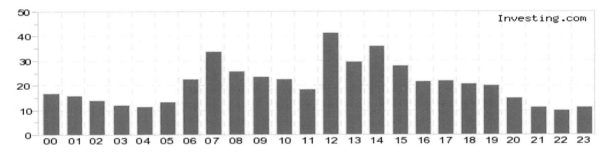

EUR/USD - Hourly Volatility (Pips/GMT Hours Source: Investing.com

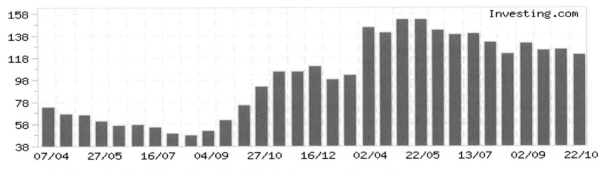

EUR/USD - Daily Volatility (In Pips) Source: Investing.com

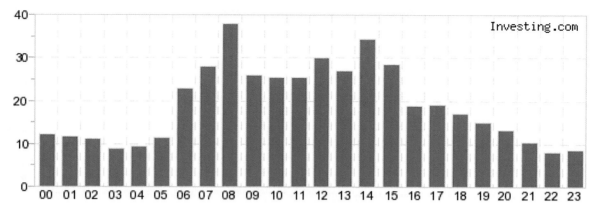

GBP/USD - Hourly Volatility (Pips/GMT Hours) Source: Investing.com

Like in the Fiber case, even the Cable is more volatile between 7 am and 8 am and between 12 am to 3 pm, moving from 25 up to 40 pips per hour. A substantial difference is evident with the Asian currencies as the NZD/JPY. By virtue of the time zone, in fact, the Asian currencies report the highest peaks of volatility during the European night.

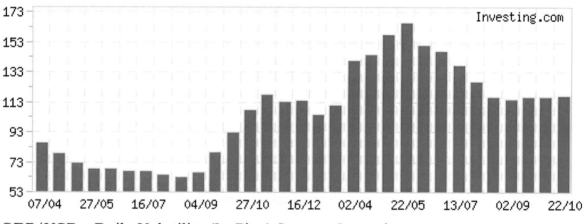

GBP/USD - Daily Volatility (In Pips) Source: Investing.com

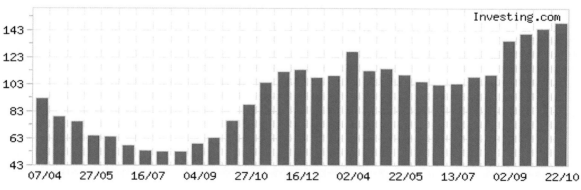

NZD/JPY - Daily Volatility (In Pips) Source: Investing.com

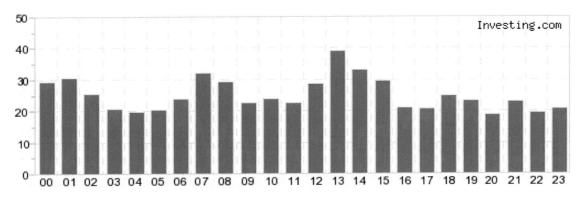

NZD/JPY - Hourly Volatility (Pips/GMT Hours)

Source: Investing.com

A difference verifiable in relation to the Fiber and Cable is that the average hourly variation is almost constant during the day. During the reporting period the variation is between 20 and 30 pips.

Holy Grail rule number 13:

Apply a breakout trading strategy during the most volatile time of the day and when both New York and London are open. Apply a range trading strategy when the volatility is low and during the mostly quiet time of the day. As George Soros pointed out, when the volatility is extremely high, a reverse should be expected. *When volatility decreases, a new trend may be forming.*

"I don't trust mutes. By their silence, I wonder what they're hiding. The lost Templar treasure, mysteries of the universe, my love for you—who knows what they could have hidden away."

Jarod Kintz

"The goal of a successful trader is to make the best trades. Money is

secondary." -

Alexander Elder

Traders can analyze multiple time frames to get deeper information for their analysis. In other words, a trader identifies the overall trend on the highest time frame and then set up the entry on the lowest one. The goal is to consider the overall market direction analyzing the longest term chart. A trader, then, can use the shortest time frame to enter a trade once the same trend it is detected. For instance, while the weekly and the daily charts are useful as an overviews on the underlying trend, the four hours and the one hour charts may be used to set up the entries. The charts from below show how the Greenback moved against the Norwegian Krone in four different time frames. Both the weekly and the daily charts show how the US Dollar is stronger than the Norwegian Krone. In particular, chart 46 shows how the price was moving slightly higher in 2014, finding a horizontal resistance at 6.30. The following break out of the resistance has projected the price to the current level at 8.40.

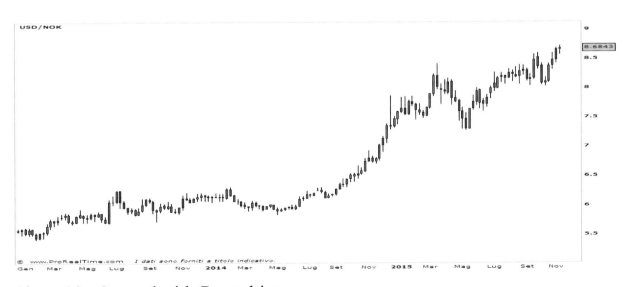

Chart 46 - Created with Prorealtime

Chart 47 shows the pair trend on a daily time frame. Again, we can see a smooth uptrend with a formation of a series of higher-highs and higher-lows. The uptrend is then clearly visible on both the long-term charts. As a result, by analyzing the four and the one-hour time-frame charts, a trader should only trigger long positions, since they have a greater chance of being profitable and they can provide a greater number of pips than the short positions. However, how can a trader open a position analyzing the four-hour and the one- hour time-frame charts? This is a discretionary choice, since it possible to evaluate different alternatives. Using the analyzed indicators, a trader could open a long trade once the RSI or the CCI move into an overbought area, or more simply, when the chart shows breakouts. In the last scenario, the long trades are opened when the price breaks out the resistance, identified on the four hours or on the one- hour time-frame charts.

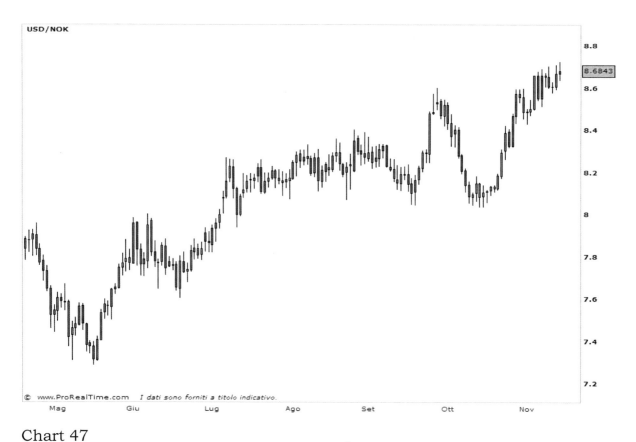

Chart 47

Created with Prorealtime

Looking at the four-hours chart, various entry points are conceivable. The first is indicated by a long white candle, whose body shows an increased volatility, between the 22th and 23rd of October. A second hypothetical entry signal is generated between the 26th and 28th of the same month, after the formation of a small horizontal resistance. The price broke such a resistance before retesting it, eventually continuing to move upwards. Between the 4th and 5th of November, the chart shows a new break to the upside, which has been proven to be a fake signal, since a long black candle subsequently pushed the price downward. A decisive upward signal, instead, was generated on November the 7th.

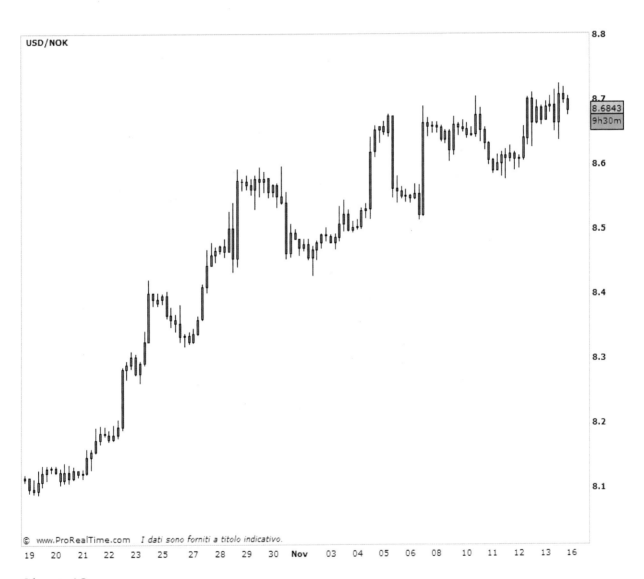

Chart 48

Created with Prorealtime

Analyzing the one-hour chart, the entry signals are less clear, even though the price moved upward.

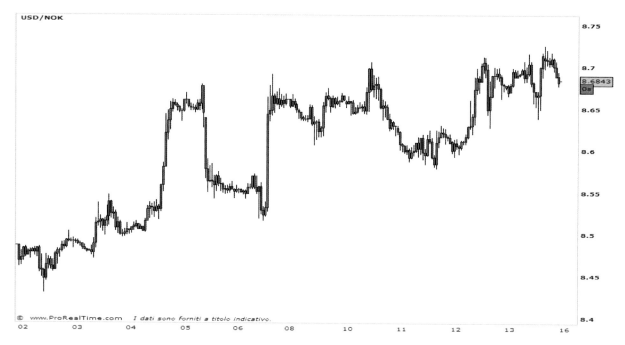

Chart 49

Created with Prorealtime

Increasing the chances of trading the correct side of the market is not the only reason why a trader should analyze different time frames. This methodology, in fact, reduces the risk, since it is possible to place tight stop losses. For instance, trading a weekly chart, retail traders may not afford to place a stop loss under a low in an uptrend. Considering the weekly chart of the example, a logical stop loss would be placed under the low at 7.30. In a four hours and one- hour time-frame charts, instead, the stop loss would be placed respectively at 8.40 and at 8.55. It is a big improvement in terms of risk prevention. Obviously, placing a stop loss below a low in a weekly chart reduces the possibility of being stopped out, since in case of retracement, the price would have more room to resume the uptrend. However, if the trend changes direction, setting a stop loss in a weekly time-frame chart would lead to a significant loss.

Let us now apply a multi time frame analysis to the AUD/NZD cross. The specific example will show how different the trends are. Chart 50 shows how the cross pair moved on one- hour time-frame chart. Clearly, it shows an uptrend, as the Australian Dollar got stronger against the New Zealand Dollar, moving from 1.0580 to almost 1.09. The study of this chart might induce the trader to open a long trade.

Chart 50

Created with Prorealtime

So, if we extend the time horizon and have a look at the four- hour time-frame chart, shown in chart 51, we see that this chart provides the same indication. Between the 11th and 17th of February, the Australian Dollar appreciated against the New Zealand Dollar. During the following days, the uptrend has undergone through a short phase of retracing, which cannot be considered as a downtrend. So far, the two charts have shown the same trend. The trader could then be tempted to open a long trade at the break of the high at 1.09.

Chart 51

Created with Prorealtime

The analysis of the daily chart can help the trader to verify if the overall trend is moving upward as well. The trader would then acquire a greater confidence about the real trend. However, the daily chart shows a great uncertainty. In fact, From May to July, the Australian Dollar appreciated sharply against the New Zealand Dollar; after that it began to move downward. Over a year, the pair oscillated from the parity to 1.18, quoting now in the middle of the range. The trend is not clear, and triggering a long trade would be then risky. In order to better understand the overall trend, it is then necessary to analyze the weekly chart. It finally clarifies what the main trend during the past few years was. What chart 53 shows is surprising. The underlying trend is downward. The uptrend, which occurred between May and July 2015, was just a retracement of the prevailing long-term downtrend. In other words, a trader who has triggered a long trade, based on the analysis of the two short time frames chart, has traded against the main trend. Obviously, it is possible to generate a profit only when the trade is performed at the right time; on the other hand, if the timing is wrong, the result would be a loss.

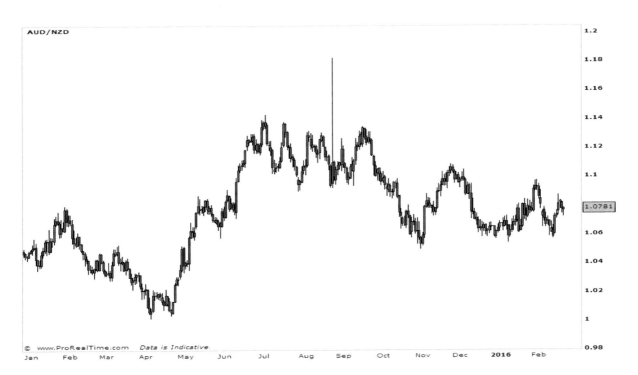

Chart 52

Created with Prorealtime

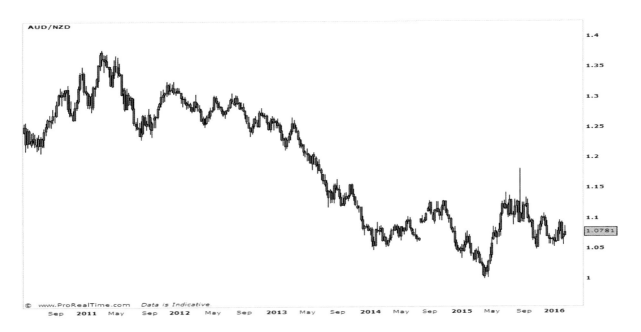

Chart 53

Created with Prorealtime

In conclusion, while the analysis of lower time-frame charts detected an uptrend, the one of the weekly chart detected a downtrend. In this case, it is highly recommended not to trade this pair cross, and to look for one that shows a same trend on different time frames.

The choice of analyzing these time-frame charts is not accidental. For instance, comparing a 30- minutes chart with a 1-hour chart, would make no sense, because the time periods are similar, and they would thus provide the same indications. Similarly, it makes no sense to compare a daily time-frame chart with a one-minute time frame chart, since the indications would be too different. The suggestion is thus to use a ratio of 1:4 or 1:6 between the trend and the entry chart.

Holy Grail rule number 14:

The multi time-frame analysis allows the trader to reduce the risk of trading. *The suggestion is to use a ratio of 1:4 or 1:6 between the time-frame analyzed to detect the main trend and the one used to place a trade.*

"The declared objective of the Templars, Guillaume de Tyre continues, was, "as far as their strength permitted, they should keep the roads and highways safe ... with especial regard for the protection of pilgrims."

Michael Baigent, *Holy Blood, Holy Grail*

17. Bollinger Bands

"Successful investing is anticipating the anticipations of others"- *John Maynard Keynes*

The Bollinger Bands indicator is a technical analysis tool created by John Bollinger in the eighties. The Bollinger Bands consist of a central twenty periods simple moving average and two outer bands. The outer bands are usually set 2 standard deviations above and below the middle band. Normally, the same period is used for both the middle band and the calculation of the standard deviation.

The question is: how can a trader exploit the Bollinger Bands? There are different ways to use the indicator. A first way is to trigger a long trade when the price touches the lower band, and to exit when it retraces back to the central moving average. *This strategy can be profitable in case of a low volatility, but not when the volatility is high since there is a risk to see the price tumbling further.* A second way is to buy when the price breaks above the upper band or to sell when the price falls below the lower band. *This is a great choice in case of high volatility and when the price is moving near a resistance or a support. Traders are then looking for a strong break out.* In order to better understand what the volatility expected in the market is, it is necessary to visualize whether the bands are contracting or separating from each other. In particular, if the bands contract towards each other, the volatility is low. Conversely, if the bands are widening out, the volatility is increasing. Chart 54 shows how to use the Bollinger Bands. Throughout 2013 and until the end of the 2014, the price was moving under the resistance at 13.50. The two bands were close each other and the Japanese candlesticks showed a progressive reduction of the amplitude. The reduction of the volatility under its average involves the possibility that an explosive movement may occur soon. In December 2014, the two bands started diverging from each other and a long white candle broke above the resistance, signaling the beginning of a new trend. A long white candle with an extraordinary long body and widening bands are an excellent trading signal. When both conditions are satisfied, traders should only look to trigger long positions. Vice versa, when a long black Marubozu breaks below the lower band and the bands are diverging from each other, traders should only open short positions. Chart 55 shows how to detect a new trend using the indicator. Before the breakout occurs, the price is moving in a narrow range. The Japanese candlesticks have small bodies and the two bands are close to each other. In August, the price breaks above the upper band, while the bands are diverging from each other. The result is an explosive movement upward.

Chart 54

Created with Prorealtime

This is the easiest way to trade with the Bollinger Bands. Chart 56, on the other hand, shows three examples of fake breakouts. This example shows how a trader should not follow a breakout strategy but rather apply a range trading strategy. The bands are far from each other and the Japanese candlesticks have long bodies. As stressed out in a previous chapter, in order to have a price explosion, it is always necessary to see a period of a low volatility. Given that the volatility is high, the best way to trade is undoubtedly to buy lows and sell highs.

The following tables show how the daily average variations are extremely limited in Forex. This implies the adoption of different strategies, when compared to stock market. In fact, while in the stock market daily changes of several points are very common, in the currency market they are very rare and they are normally limited to a few points over a month or a year. The tables show that the Euro has lost 25 points against the US Dollar over one year; 13 over six months and 8 over one month. Expanding the time horizon to three years, the loss amounted to 20 points.

Chart 55

Created with Prorealtime

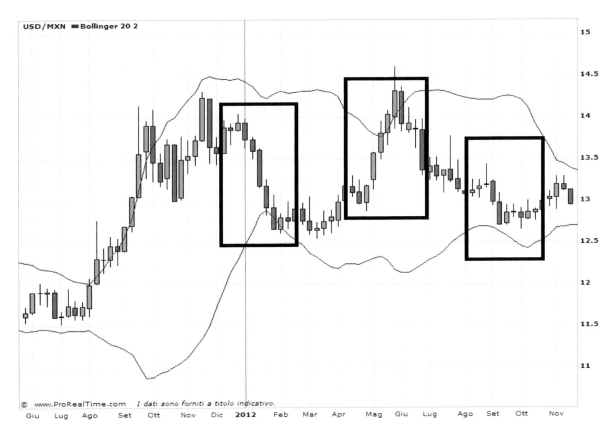

Chart 56

Created with Prorealtime

These data suggest the trader that, while it is always important to trade the correct part of the market, opening counter trend trades at the right moment is not a wrong choice. In the specific example from below, the US Dollar has shown to be the strongest currency and to register the best performance against the Norwegian and the Swedish Krone. The variation against them was approximately of 37 points over one year.

Pair	Daily	1 Week	1 Month	YTD	1 Year	3 Years
EUR/USD	-1.31%	-3.21%	-7.91%	-13.25%	-24.57%	-19.73%
GBP/USD	-0.91%	-1.93%	-4.25%	-5.32%	-11.41%	-6.09%
USD/JPY	0.09%	0.46%	2.32%	1.42%	19.76%	45.38%
USD/CHF	0.31%	1.97%	7.92%	1.15%	15.27%	8.97%
AUD/USD	-0.94%	-1.08%	-1.67%	-6.55%	-15.44%	-27.49%
USD/CAD	0.76%	1.27%	2.63%	9.99%	15.11%	28.85%
NZD/USD	-0.62%	-0.24%	-1.79%	-5.85%	-13.97%	-10.33%
USD/ZAR	1.46%	3.62%	7.08%	7.82%	16.84%	63.82%
USD/TRY	2.18%	0.58%	7.41%	13.06%	19.27%	46.94%

Table 4 - Source: Investing.com

Pair	Daily	1 Week	1 Month	YTD	1 Year	3 Years
USD/MXN	0.61%	-0.09%	3.88%	4.99%	17.23%	22.22%
USD/PLN	1.49%	3.84%	7.82%	11.56%	30.13%	25.56%
USD/SEK	1.48%	3.04%	3.63%	11.77%	36.48%	28.25%
USD/SGD	0.78%	1.08%	2.77%	5.05%	10.03%	10.15%
USD/DKK	1.36%	3.53%	8.83%	15.47%	32.47%	25.01%
USD/NOK	1.32%	3.81%	8.33%	9.83%	37.44%	41.84%

Table 5 - Source: Investing.com

It is now time to back test four different trading systems based on the analyzed indicators, such as the moving averages, the MACD, and the Bollinger Bands. The first one is based on the Bollinger Bands, the second has been developed using the MACD indicator; the third one, called "Kamast brevissime", is based on a particular kind of moving averages, the so called Kama moving averages. The last one was created using a price oscillator and adopting a take profit. The back test is applied on EUR/USD and over a period of nine years. The four trading systems are tested using a capital of $10,000, with no reinvestment of the profits, and trading only one lot per time. No stop losses have been used and all the trades have been closed reversing the position. The reader should be aware that, as with other back tests based on past data, the results are not indicative of an equal future performance. Let us now analyze how the first trading system performed. The expert advisor is back tested on a daily chart, and it is based exclusively on the Bollinger Bands. No other filters were added in order to verify the effectiveness of the indicator and the outcome is positive. More in detail, the system is profitable in 38.22 % of the trades. It generated 157 trades, of which 67 are winners and 95 losers. The maximum drawdown is of 24.190 dollars against a maximum run up of 64.110 dollars.

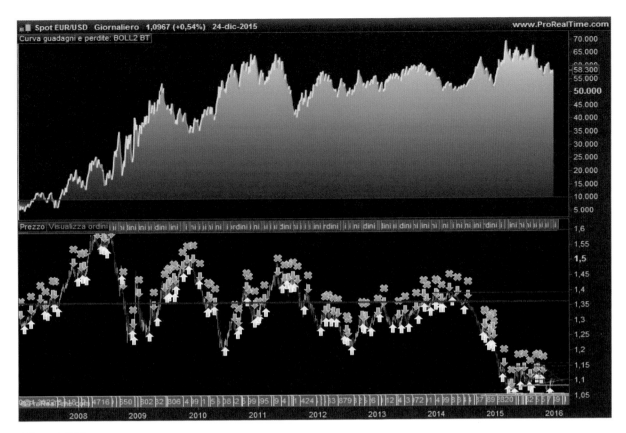

Chart 57

Created with Prorealtime

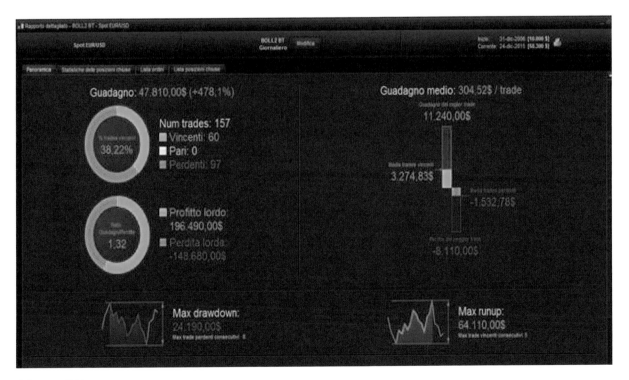

Chart 58

Created with Prorealtime

The average profit per trade is 3274.83 dollars against an average loss of $1532.78. The trading system is therefore successful, as the profit/loss ratio is 1.32. Over the analyzed period, the expert advisor has generated a return of + 478 %, with a final profit of $47.810. As mentioned at the beginning of the book, the best way to make profits is not to take the profits too soon and to let them run as much as possible. In this sense, although the expert advisor is winning less than 4 times out of 10, it is yet profitable, since the winning trades guarantee an average gain much higher than the average loss.

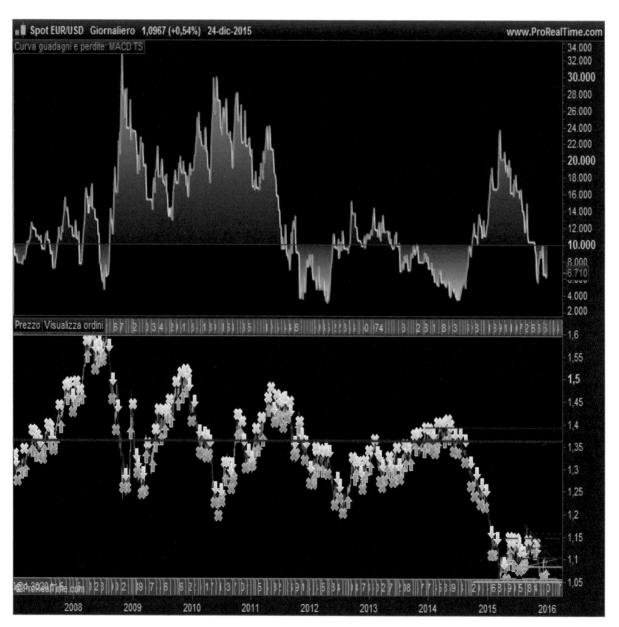

Chart 59

Data with Prorealtime

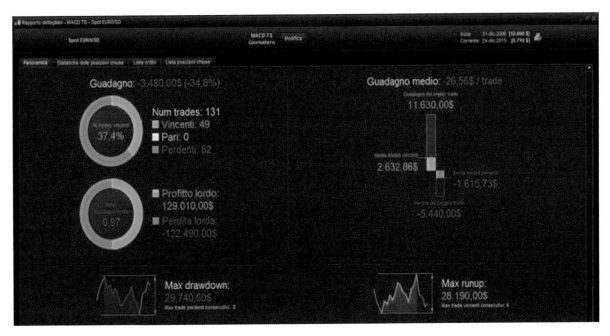

Chart 60

Created with Prorealtime

The trading system based on the use of the MACD has generated a loss
of 3480 dollars. The profit/loss ratio is equal to 0.97. The system delivered 49
profitable trades against 82 losing trades. The maximum drawdown is 29740
dollars against a maximum run up of 28190 dollars. The equity curve
displayed in the upper section of chart 57 shows a random movement,
suggesting that the MACD has performed poorly. Over all, the result is a loss
of $ 3480. The "kamast brevissime" expert advisor was developed using a
particular kind of moving averages, the so called Kama moving averages.
Developed by Perry Kaufman, the indicator is calculated using a volatility
ratio. The great advantage of the kama system is that it generates fewer fake
signals in comparison to the classic moving averages. The trading system has
performed better than the previous one with a max drawdown of 17.100
dollars against a max run up of 126.170 dollars. The profit/loss ratio is 3.17
and the number of profitable trades is higher than the number of losing
trades. In fact, the total amount of trades generated is 41, with 22 winners
and 19 losers. The final result is a profit of 102.320$, or a + 1023.20%. Chart
64 shows the results of a trading system based on a price oscillator with a
take profit. Over all, this trading system generated a good result. Yet, it is

appropriate to mention the high discretion in the calculation of the take profit, since the results vary considerably on the basis of the percentage of profit that has been set. Obviously the use of a take profit increased the percentage of the winning trades. The profit/loss ratio increased significantly being equal to 2.82. In other words, the gross profits are almost 3 times the losses. The maximum drawdown is of 27.460 dollars against a max run up of 81770 dollars. Over all, the system has gained a 665 %, realizing a profit of 65.650$.

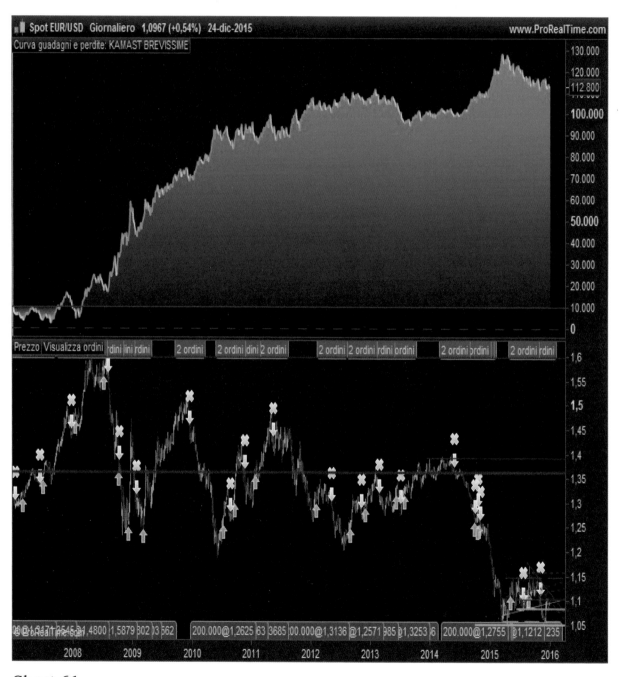

Chart 61

Created with Prorealtime

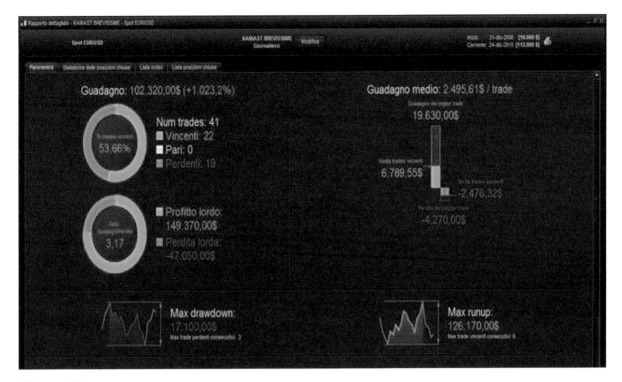

Chart 62

Created with Prorealtime

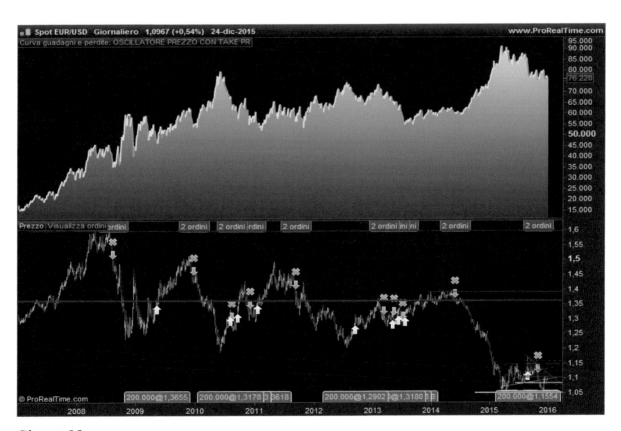

Chart 63

Created with Prorealtime

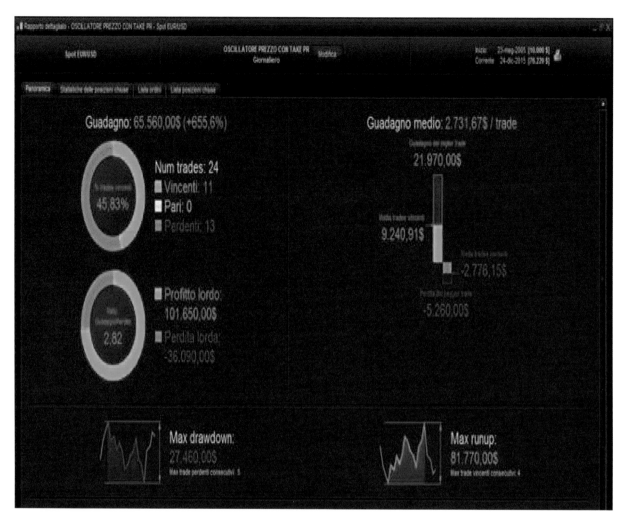

Chart 64

Created with Prorealtime

Holy Grail rule number 15:

A very low volatility along with the Bollinger Bands moving really close to each other may be the sign that a larger movement is imminent. Be then ready to *trade breakouts if the price is starting to move close to a resistance or a support and the Bollinger Bands are starting to diverge from each other.* Conversely, *buy lows and sell highs if the Bollinger Bands are far from each other and the candlesticks have long bodies.* Do not rely on trading systems based on classic indicators. The results vary too much according to the indicator used and to the analyzed cross.

"May the spirit which once inhabited this skull rise up and testify against me, if ever I willfully violate my obligation of a Knight Templar."

Martin Short, Inside the brotherhood

18. Fundamental Analysis

"The market does not know if you are long or short and could not care less. You are the only one emotionally involved with your position. The market is just reacting to supply and demand and if you are cheering it one way, there is always somebody else cheering it just as hard that it will go the other way"-*Marty Schwartz*

Technical analysts try to forecast how a currency might move in the future through the analysis of past data. Fundamentalists, on the other hand, look at macro-economic data-sets to achieve the same purpose, believing that the economic and the political changes of a nation can generate considerable variations on the underlying currency. The Growth Domestic Product, the Inflation Rate and some other estimations all have a strong impact on the underlying currency, generating large fluctuations which may move the currency towards a new balance. Central Bankers focus on the most important data for a nation's economy in order to evaluate where and if moving the base rate, with inflation and employment two of the most studied data-sets, both by the central bankers and the forex traders. When the unemployment statistics are released, traders will price it with a probability of a possible rate hike or a cut by Central Bankers. When the inflation data is released, traders will incorporate it into prices, while Central Bankers will monitor the statistics to decide what action they might be taking at the next meeting. Normally, growing unemployment and decreasing inflation can induce the Central Bankers to consider a rate cut. Over time, new statistical methods have been devised to anticipate changes to inflation, unemployment and interest rates. In particular, the consumer statistics are important since they provide an insight into the real economy. Since the consumer activity is considered as a precursor to inflation and growth, these data is analyzed by traders very carefully. A higher degree of volatility can be observed around the time of the release of Consumer Sentiment Numbers. Moreover, traders focus on production numbers, even more so lately, when it comes to emerging economies, propelling the global growth. China is the main example. The 'PMI' (Purchasing Managers Index), which is released every month, drives a global interest among investors. The Purchasing Managers Index is the result of a survey recorded among producers, which express their sentiment on future orders. So, if the producers are receiving more orders than expected, it is more likely the economic cycle is improving; while if the producers are receiving fewer orders than expected, that might point towards an upcoming contraction in the economic cycle. Below, we will study the most important fundamental variables more in depth.

- **GDP**: It stands for Growth Domestic Product. It is an estimate of a nation's production and consumption of goods and services. A strong GDP number may generate an increase in the demand for the nation's currency. Traders monitor this figure closely, and its release is usually accompanied by an increased volatility, especially if it upsets the expectations. If the growth is positive and above expectations, the underlying currency usually tends to appreciate, while on the opposite case, the currency tends to depreciate. Over time, a strong economic expansion can affect the inflation rate and it might induce the National Central Bank to increase the interest rate.

- **CENTRAL BANKS AND INTEREST RATE**: Central Banks are responsible for supervising the monetary system of a nation. They manage the monetary policy to ensure the stability, while maintaining or achieving a low inflation rate. They are also responsible of regulating the credit system, controlling the exchange reserves and to finally to oversee the commercial banks. Central banks can influence the level of the economic activity, acting on the base rate. The base rate is the interest which the Central Banks apply to commercial banks. Normally, central banks reduce the base rate to help the economy to recover from a recession or a prolonged period of a slow growth, while they increase the base rate when the economy is overheated.

- **TRADE BALANCE**: also known as the balance of trade (BOT), is an estimate of a country's exports minus its imports. When the imports are larger than the exports, a country has a trade deficit. When exports are larger than imports, a country has a trade surplus. A country with a large trade deficit needs to borrow money to purchase goods and services, while a country with a trade surplus can lend money to deficit countries. The trade balance helps to understand the strength of a country's economy when compared to other countries. An increasing account deficit or a high deficit is associated to a weaker currency.

- **INFLATION RATE**: also named CPI, Consumer and Producer Price Index. CPI is the headline figure for inflation. The index assesses the changes in the price of a basket of goods and it represents a decline in the purchasing power. The figure includes several categories of goods and services like: housing, transportation, food, medical care, education and communication, apparel, and others. The figure is released every month, either a month over month, or as percentage change for the entire year. If a nation is experiencing a higher inflation than expected, the Central Bank may be inclined to increase the rate of interest. Conversely, if the inflation is lower than estimated, the Central Bank might reduce the interest rate.

- **UNEMPLOYMENT RATE**: It represents the percentage of the total labor force which is unemployed at a given time. High unemployment means also lower wages and overall a reduced consumer spending. As a consequence, a high or a rising unemployment might put pressure on interest rates. Simply put, Central banks might reduce the interest rate to stimulate the growth, with the effect to create new jobs.

- **THE UNIVERSITY OF MICHIGAN CONSUMER SENTIMENT INDEX**: It estimates the consumer confidence regarding the business conditions and the purchasing power, based on phone surveys. It is evaluated as the main indicator of the US consumer sentiment and it is used to predict future economic downturns. In fact, if the consumer confidence is decreasing, it might be seen a drop in the real consumer spending.

- **USD ADVANCE RETAIL SALES:** It is an estimate of sales of goods to retail clients. The figure is quite important since the consumer spending counts for more than two-thirds of the whole US economy. One third of such spending is given by the retail sales. However, retail sales can change a lot due to seasonality; in other words, the figure can be positive one month, to be negative the month later.

Normally, a data release is associated to an increased volatility. Fundamentalists do not necessarily trade after a data is released. They normally need to overview different data-sets and only after they take positions. Technical analysts do the opposite and, in particular, breakout traders are the most active as the volatility increases around the most important data release time. The point is that to be profitable, both fundamental and technical analysis can be used. In fact, there is no a dichotomy between the two methods. Traders should always have an overview of the economy of the nation which the underlying currency refer to and an idea on the development of possible future scenarios. A concrete example can help to understand better how to use both the analyses. The United States is the world's largest economy. Over 2015, the GDP grew by about 2%, with the unemployment rate below 5%. At the end of 2015, the Central Bank raised the interest rate and it has implied that would raise further four times over the course of 2016. After the 2008/2009 recession, the economy, although it did not climb quickly, still managed to grow and to create new jobs. Both elements favored the rise of the US Dollar. In fact, the expectation of higher interest rates pushed up the US Dollar against the other currencies also during 2015. The fundamental analysis therefore suggests that the best way to trade the currency is to only trigger long positions. Technical analysis can be then used to open a position with the best risk/reward ratio. However, in March 2016, Yellen, the President of the US Central Bank, stated that the change in the base rate will no longer be carried out over a four but two sessions. Obviously no one knows the extent of the rate increase, whenever they will decide to increase it during the two events scheduled on the agenda. However, the expectation of a smaller increase in the annual base rate, provoked a reaction with the US Dollar, which devalued against the other major currencies. The fundamental analysis therefore requires the trader to rethink about the possible strength of the US Dollar. Technically, the long-term trend is not invalidated, but the trader is now aware that a reverse is possible in the short or medium term. Since a nation's economy is not static but dynamic, central bankers need to evaluate all statistics continuously and they can change their vision on how use the levers at all times. In other words, the fundamental analysis cannot be ignored. It would be like a fatal mistake for a short-sighted driver to do so without wearing glasses. Another concrete example can clarify the importance of regular follow the fundamental analysis. In January 2016, there was a sharp decline in share prices in the various global lists, as a result of continued reductions in growth expectations in China. The turbulence in the equity markets coincided with the appreciation of the Japanese Yen and the Swiss Franc. In particular, since 2013, the Japanese Yen moved in a strong downtrend against the US Dollar. However, it is probably now in place a final inversion of the trend, which can also be supported by the study of technical analysis. The study of what happened in the past can help the trader to predict what can happen when stock markets go down. The table below shows what happened in 2008, when the world economy fell into repression. When stock markets turn down, the currencies which tend to appreciate are generally the Japanese Yen and the Swiss Franc. In particular, in 2008, the currencies that appreciated more were the Japanese Yen, the Swiss Franc, then the US Dollar and finally the Euro. On the other hand, the currencies that underwent a significant depreciation are the Australian Dollar, the British Pound and the New Zealand Dollar.

Currency		Grow / Fall
JPY		42.9 %
CHF		20.98 %
USD		13.66 %
EUR		9.34 %
CAD		-10.15 %
AUD		-11.1 %
GBP		-11.79 %
NZD		-16.97 %

Table 6 - Source: Tradingeconomics.com

The tables below illustrate the most important indicators for eighteen countries.

Unemployment Rate

	Last		Previous	Highest	Lowest			
United States	4.90	Jan/16	5	10.8	2.5	%	Monthly	
Euro Area	10.40	Dec/15	10.5	12.1	7.2	%	Monthly	
China	4.05	Dec/15	4.05	4.3	3.9	%	Quarterly	
Japan	3.30	Dec/15	3.3	5.6	1	%	Monthly	
Germany	4.50	Dec/15	4.5	14.2	0.4	%	Monthly	
United Kingdom	5.10	Nov/15	5.2	12	3.4	%	Monthly	
France	10.60	Sep/15	10.4	10.8	7.2	%	Quarterly	
Brazil	6.90	Dec/15	7.5	13.1	4.3	%	Monthly	
Italy	11.40	Dec/15	11.4	13	5.8	%	Monthly	
India	4.90	Dec/13	5.2	9.4	4.9	%	Yearly	
Russia	5.80	Dec/15	5.8	14.1	4.8	%	Monthly	
Canada	7.20	Jan/16	7.1	13.1	2.9	%	Monthly	
Australia	5.80	Dec/15	5.8	11.1	4	%	Monthly	
South Korea	3.40	Dec/15	3.4	7.1	2.9	%	Monthly	
Spain	20.90	Dec/15	21.18	26.94	4.41	%	Quarterly	

	Last		Previous	Highest	Lowest		
Mexico	3.96	Dec/15	3.96	5.93	2.22	%	Monthly
Indonesia	6.18	Sep/15	5.94	11.24	2	%	Quarterly
Netherlands	6.60	Dec/15	6.7	7.9	3.6	%	Monthly

Table 7 - Source: Tradingeconomics.com

Interest Rate

	Last		Previous	Highest	Lowest		
United States	0.50	Jan/16	0.5	20	0.25	%	Daily
Euro Area	0.05	Jan/16	0.05	4.75	0.05	%	Daily
China	4.35	Jan/16	4.6	10.98	4.6	%	Daily
Japan	-0.10	Jan/16	0	9	-0.1	%	Daily
Germany	0.05	Jan/16	0.05	4.75	0.05	%	Daily
United Kingdom	0.50	Feb/16	0.5	17	0.5	%	Daily
France	0.05	Jan/16	0.05	4.75	0.05	%	Daily
Brazil	14.25	Jan/16	14.25	45	7.25	%	Daily
Italy	0.05	Jan/16	0.05	4.75	0.05	%	Daily
India	6.75	Feb/16	7.25	14.5	4.25	%	Daily
Russia	11.00	Jan/16	11	17	5	%	Daily
Canada	0.50	Jan/16	0.5	16	0.25	%	Daily
Australia	2.00	Feb/16	2	17.5	2	%	Daily
South Korea	1.50	Jan/16	1.5	5.25	1.5	%	Daily
Spain	0.05	Jan/16	0.05	4.75	0.05	%	Daily
Mexico	3.25	Feb/16	3.25	9.25	3	%	Daily
Indonesia	7.25	Jan/16	7.5	12.75	5.75	%	Daily
Netherlands	0.05	Jan/16	0.05	4.75	0.05	%	Daily

Table 8 - Source: Tradingeconomics.com

Inflation Rate

	Last		Previous	Highest	Lowest			
United States	0.70	Dec/15	0.5	23.7	-15.8	%	Monthly	
Euro Area	0.40	Jan/16	0.2	5	-0.7	%	Monthly	
China	1.60	Dec/15	1.5	28.4	-2.2	%	Monthly	
Japan	0.20	Dec/15	0.3	25	-2.52	%	Monthly	
Germany	0.50	Jan/16	0.3	11.54	-7.62	%	Monthly	
United Kingdom	0.20	Dec/15	0.1	8.5	-0.1	%	Monthly	
France	0.20	Jan/16	0.2	18.8	-0.7	%	Monthly	
Brazil	10.71	Jan/16	10.67	6821	1.65	%	Monthly	
Italy	0.30	Jan/16	0.1	25.64	-0.6	%	Monthly	
India	5.69	Jan/16	5.61	11.16	3.69	%	Monthly	
Russia	9.80	Jan/16	12.9	2333	3.6	%	Monthly	
Canada	1.60	Dec/15	1.4	21.6	-17.8	%	Monthly	
Australia	1.70	Dec/15	1.5	23.9	-1.3	%	Quarterly	
South Korea	0.80	Jan/16	1.3	32.5	0.2	%	Monthly	
Spain	-0.30	Jan/16	0	28.43	-1.37	%	Monthly	
Mexico	2.61	Jan/16	2.13	180	2.13	%	Monthly	
Indonesia	4.14	Jan/16	3.35	82.4	-1.17	%	Monthly	
Netherlands	0.60	Jan/16	0.7	11.19	-1.3	%	Monthly	

Table 9 - Source: Tradingeconomics.com

GDP Annual Growth Rate

	Last		Previous	Highest	Lowest			
United States	1.80	Dec/15	2.1	13.4	-4.1	%	Quarterly	
Euro Area	1.50	Dec/15	1.6	5	-5.6	%	Quarterly	
China	6.80	Dec/15	6.9	15.4	3.8	%	Quarterly	
Japan	1.60	Sep/15	0.7	9.4	-9.4	%	Quarterly	

	Last		Previous	Highest	Lowest			
Germany	2.10	Dec/15	1.8	6	-7.9	%	Quarterly	
United Kingdom	1.90	Dec/15	2.1	9.8	-5.9	%	Quarterly	
France	1.50	Dec/15	1.1	12.5	-3.95	%	Quarterly	
Brazil	-4.50	Sep/15	-3	10.1	-4.5	%	Quarterly	
Italy	1.00	Dec/15	0.8	10.3	-7.2	%	Quarterly	
India	7.30	Dec/15	7.4	11.4	-5.2	%	Quarterly	
Russia	-3.80	Dec/15	-4.1	12.1	-11.2	%	Quarterly	
Canada	1.20	Sep/15	1.1	8.8	-4.1	%	Quarterly	
Australia	2.50	Sep/15	2	9	-3.4	%	Quarterly	
South Korea	3.00	Dec/15	2.7	18.2	-7.3	%	Quarterly	
Spain	3.50	Dec/15	3.4	5.6	-4.3	%	Quarterly	
Mexico	2.50	Dec/15	2.6	8.5	-8.1	%	Quarterly	
Indonesia	5.04	Dec/15	4.73	7.16	1.56	%	Quarterly	
Netherlands	1.60	Dec/15	1.9	6.1	-4.9	%	Quarterly	

Table: 10 - Source: Tradingeconomics.com

Holy Grail rule number 16:

What drives major players is not the rate applied at a given time, but the expectation about its possible reduction or increase. A trader should always have an overview of the economy of the country to which the currency refers to. Traders needs to be flexible since the economy of a nation is never stable and it implies a continuous rethinking about future scenarios. Historically, during bear stock markets, the Swiss Franc and the Japanese Yen tend to appreciate.

"The gods know what's important, what's wrong about you. They know everything. If you go out searching for the Holy Grail, they won't let you find it."

Tom Spanbauer, *In the City of Shy Hunters*

19. Market sentiment – C.O.T. report

"Bull markets are born on pessimism, grow on skepticism, mature on optimism, and die on euphoria. The time of maximum pessimism is the best time to buy, and the time of maximum optimism is the best time to sell. If you want to have a better performance than the crowd, you must do things differently from crowd." *–John Templeton*

Traders wanting to know how the major market players are positioned can analyze the open interest in the futures' and the options' markets. The open interest refers to the number of contracts entered and not yet offset. In particular, the open interest increases by one unit when a new buyer enters in the market a new purchase order and a seller a new sell order. It is important to specify that when a buyer purchases from a previous buyer who intends to sell, there is no increase in the open interest. The open interest data are updated by the commitment of traders (C.O.T.) on a weekly basis. They report the open interest for the currencies where twenty or more traders hold positions exceeding a given threshold. Furthermore, the report makes a relevant distinction between commercials and non-commercials positions. For the most part, the commercials are the producers, while the non-commercials are the large speculators. The question arises on how can retail traders benefit from the information contained in the Cot report. Firstly, a growing open interest should be read as a confirmation of the trend in progress, whereas a decrease is a warning for a trend which might be close to its end. As shown in the charts below, the commercials are always on the opposite side of the market except when the trend is nearing its end. Conversely, being trend followers, the large speculators trade the correct side of market, with the exception of when trend is at the end.

The **Commitments of Traders Report** is split into three groups:

- Commercials: Producer/Merchant/Processor/User and Swap Dealers
- Non-Commercials or Large Speculators: Managed Money and Other Reportables
- Small Speculators

Therefore, when large traders are net long and small traders are net short, the market is bullish and a trader should only look to open long trades. *The larger the relative net short position of the small traders, the stronger is the bullish trend.* However, if the two-week trend in the large trader position is moving down, or in other words, if the large trades are closing their net long position, a trader should liquidate all long positions as well, since this is a warning sign that the trend may be close to its end. Conversely, if large traders are holding a net short position with small trader net long, the market is bearish. *The larger the relative long position of the small traders, the stronger is the bearish trend.* However, if the two-week trend in the large trader position is moving up or, in other words, if the large trades are closing their net short position, a trader should liquidate all short positions as well. These rules are generally valid, but it is always appropriate to monitor the market constantly, since it might happen that retail traders can hit the correct direction of the market, as it happened with T-bonds markets recently. It is also appropriate that the COT report including both futures and options confirm the futures only report. Chart 65 shows how the Australian Dollar moved against the US Dollar over three years. The couple tumbled from 1.05 to 0.70. The chart shows six macro trends. In particular, during 2012 and along 2013, the pair moved in range between 0.95 and 1.05. During this period, the large traders were long with the exception of the beginning of summer 2012, when they have temporarily reversed their longs, opening short trades. However, the commercials were extremely short with the exception of the aforementioned period. It is interesting to see what happened in August 2013, when the large traders closed their longs to reverse into short positions. Technically, the pair found a support at 0.95. The trend changed definitively with the break out of the support at 0.95. When large traders reverse their positions, this may be a signal that the trend could change soon and it may be close to its end. In fact, the large traders have the tendency to add long positions in a bullish trend or to add short positions in a bearish trend, generating a bullish or a bearish sentiment extreme. What happened is that the pair retested the former support - with a resistance at 0.95, to then continue to move down. With the exception of the spring and summer 2014, the trend was definitely oriented downward. It is important to note that traders should always keep attention to the extreme thresholds. In other words, when large traders and commercials hold extremely far positions, a short-term trend change is to be expected. From a technical standpoint, what happens is that the profitable traders close their positions in a profit, while even the last traders, which were holding a losing position, are stopped. Chart 66 shows the Fiber trend over a year. The pair depreciated from 1.20 until 1.06. The large speculators perfectly followed the downtrend of the pair. A first extreme is detected in early January when the large traders and the commercials have found themselves on extreme opposite ends. This coincided with a timid bounce. However, the downtrend continued until March. From March onwards, the large traders have reversed their short positions, starting to buy Euros against Us Dollars. From a technical viewpoint, between March and April, a small double bottom was formed, from which the price then bounced. From May until November, the large speculators held long positions while commercials reversed the position becoming net short. In that phase, the Fiber moved in a range. Neither of the two forces was capable to overcome the other one. A further reversal of the positions occurred in November, when large speculators reversed their positions becoming short on the pair. Chart 67 shows the evolution of the cable over the course of two years. Three macro trends are detectable, perfectly followed by the positions of large traders. The first uptrend ended between July and August 2014, when the large traders reversed their positions becoming net short. The movement downwards lasted until May 2015, when the large trader again reversed their positions becoming net long.

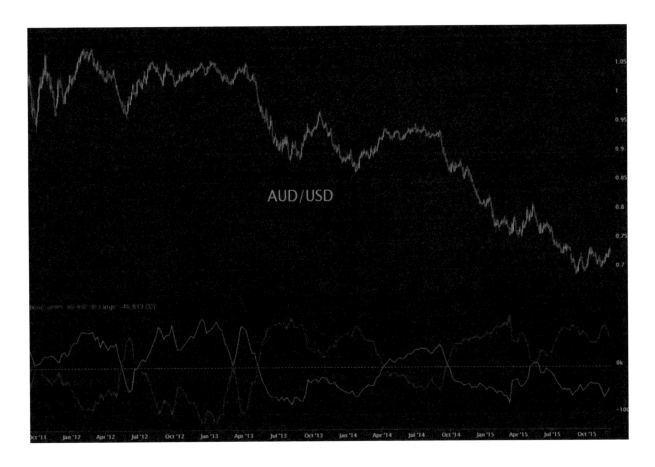

Chart 65 - Source: Timingcharts.com

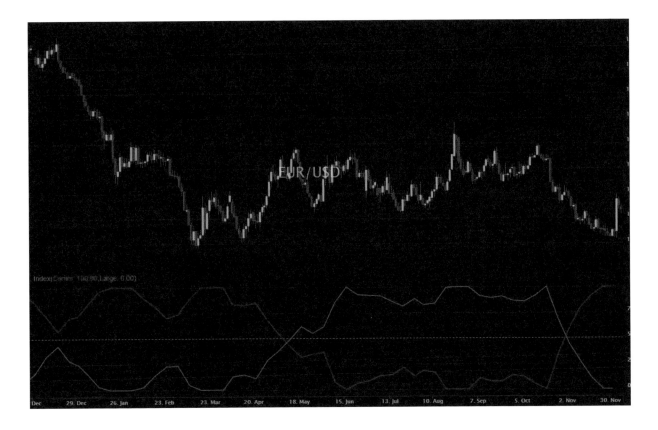

Chart 66 - Source: Timingcharts.com

The latest movement was an uptrend over the summer, only to then lose directionality. The last example, shown in chart 68, refers to Japanese Yen. It shows a smooth downtrend, where the commercials were net long for almost three years. Conversely, the large traders were net short for the same period of time. This example perfectly shows how it is important to study how the big players are positioned in the market.

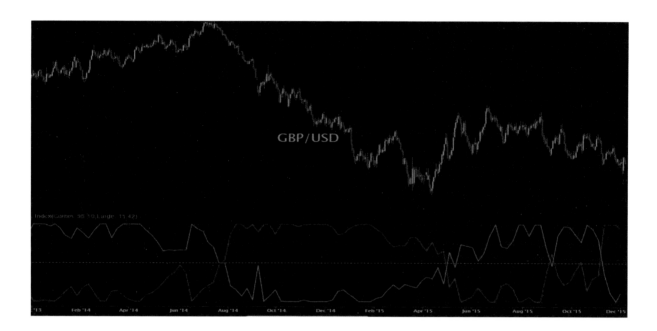

Chart 67 - Source: Timingcharts.com

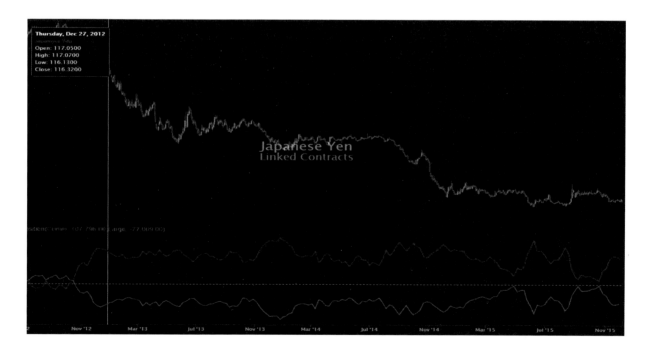

Chart 68 - Source: Timingcharts.com

Holy Grail rule number 17:

Traders can forecast a future currency trend looking at how large traders and commercials are positioned in the market. While large traders tend to trade the correct part of the market, commercials hedge their trades, resulting then on the opposite side of the market. However, when the two opposite sides of market reach an extreme level, a trend reverse is expected.

"Sweet brother, I have seen the Holy Grail...

The Holy Thing is here again

Among us, brother, fast thou too and pray,

And tell thy brother knights to fast and pray,

That so perchance the vision may be seen

By thee and those, and all the world be healed."

Alfred, Lord Tennyson, *Idylls of the King*

20. Money Management

"I am more concerned about controlling the downside. Learn to take the losses. The most important thing about making money is not to let your losses get out of hand"- *Marty Schwartz*

One of the main reason why the retail traders lose money is that they do not always use the appropriate money-management techniques. As it was explained in chapter one, the way a trade is managed accounts for a great deal of any profits. The main difference between professionals and retail traders is that the first cut their losses quickly, while the retails traders tend to do the opposite, cutting winners short and letting losing trades run out of control. The ability to make profits and close the losing trades is not the only key difference between the two categories of traders. For example, while the professional traders only use a small portion of their accounts per single trade, the retail traders usually trade a larger portion of their accounts. Professional traders usually do not use more than 2% of the entire capital per trade. Statistics suggest that the retail traders tend to use instead a much bigger size per trade. Since brokers allow them to use the leverage, they are encouraged to open large size trades, using a relatively small capital. *However, the higher is the leverage used, the larger are the potential losses.* In other words, the retail traders are risking more than they might be able to afford. An in depth, a study conducted by a main broker revealed that retail traders have the best chance of being profitable after 1 year of trading, when using a leverage ratio of 5:1 or smaller. A 5:1 leverage ratio means that a trader can open a position for $ 50.000, using $ 10.000. The same research demonstrated that the possibilities of being profitable in one year, decrease dramatically when using a higher leverage. In other words, higher leverage ratios are linked to a higher probability to hit a loss. The reason is that when trading with an excessive leverage, the trade may not have enough space to draw down before it moves in the trader's direction. The same study revealed how retail traders were profitable 6 times out of 10 when using a leverage ratio such as 5:1 or smaller, while they were profitable less than 5 times out of 10 when using a leverage ratio such as 25:1 or higher. These data are evidence enough that an excessive leverage works against the trader. The following is a list of the most common rules that professional traders generally follow.

1. Maximum risk per trade is typically around 2-3%.

2. Two lots per trade.

3. Two different targets for each trade. First lot is closed at first target.

4. Once the first target is hit, stop loss is moved to the entry point for the second lot.

A classic way to manage a trade is to trail the stop up or down every time a new position is added, in order not to risk more than a predetermined amount. However, retail traders are often confused about when it is appropriate to add a new position. The answer is that it may be appropriate to scale into a winning position only when the market is trending strongly, since there are no logical reasons to scale in when the market is moving in a choppy way. Once a new position is added, it is important to trail the stop on the previous position. In this way, the first position is at breakeven and the risk is now pending on the second one. Another main reason why the retail traders are not profitable is because the average account size. It is extremely important to not trade if the account size is limited. Simply put, if the trade goes against, there is a high risk of not having enough space to make the trade run, and as a consequence the trader can hit a margin call. A simple data can clarify how it is important to not trade with a limited amount of money. When trading with an average account of 1,000 $, only two traders out of 10, turned in a profit after a year. When, on the other hand, trading with 10.000 $, more than four traders out of 10, were profitable at one year. It is then important to know how much should be traded based on the available capital and the number of pips risked. The formula below is extremely useful in order to trade fair.

Position Size = (Account Size * Percent Risked) / Number of Pips Risked * Pip Value

1. **Account Size** – The amount of money in the account (Example: $5,000)

2. **Percent Risked** – The amount of risk in a percentage (Example: 2%)

3. **Number of Pips Risked** - The amount of pips between the stop loss and the entry

4. **Pip Value** - See chart below

A less common approach is called "grid trading ". It is a strategy based on placing multiple trades to form a grid pattern. The purpose is to place both long and short trades around the current price to exploit the market volatility. In this way, a trader does not need to predict the market direction. Obviously, such a trading system performs better when the volatility is high or in ranging markets. Ideally, the system works better when the price moves in a range across the entry point. Since this system opens long and short trades on the same cross, it is a *market neutral strategy.* So, when should a trader close the trades? The most obvious answer is to dynamically close out trades once they hit a profit target. However, the disadvantage of this system is that it is necessary to wait until a target is hit. That means that, meanwhile, a trader cannot manage the capital and the account margin. It is worth noting that once a certain level is reached, the order on the opposing level should be cancelled. However, the risk is to then see a losing trade get worse and worse. This strategy should be then avoided in case of strong trending markets. The grid-trading strategy is a variant of the hedging strategy. As discussed before, it is possible to hedge on the same cross, opening at the same time a long and a short trade, or to use two different cross, when there is a strong correlation between them.

PIP-VALUES (in U.S. dollars, per mini-lot) FOR 27 CURRENCY PAIRS

CURRENCY PAIR	1 PIP =
AUD/NZD	$1.00 times NZD/USD
AUD/CAD, EUR/CAD, GBP/CAD, USD/CAD	$1.00 divided by USD/CAD
AUD/JPY, CAD/JPY, CHF/JPY, EUR/JPY, GBP/JPY, NZD/JPY, USD/JPY	$100.00 divided by USD/JPY
AUD/USD, EUR/USD, GBP/USD, NZD/USD	$1.00
EUR/AUD, GBP/AUD	$1.00 times AUD/USD
EUR/CHF, GBP/CHF, USD/CHF	$1.00 divided by USD/CHF
EUR/GBP	$1.00 times GBP/USD
USD/DKK	$1.00 divided by USD/DKK
EUR/NOK, USD/NOK	$1.00 divided by USD/NOK
EUR/SEK, USD/SEK	$1.00 divided by USD/SEK

Notes

1. For standard lots, multiply pip-values by 10.

2. For micro lots, divide pip-values by 10.

3. In every case, the base-currency has no bearing on the pip-value of a pair; it is the cross-currency which determines that value. So, for example, all yen pairs have the same pip-value, because in all yen pairs the JPY is always the cross-currency.

4. To calculate the pip-value of a yen pair, we start with $100.00 (instead of $1.00) and divide it by the current price of the USD/JPY. The difference is because in all yen pairs, one pip is represented by the second decimal place in the price; whereas, in all non-yen pairs, one pip is represented by the fourth decimal place in the price.

Table: 11 - Source: Tradewithpriceaction.com

The next table provides an insight into the correlation between different crosses at 10 days.

	AUDUSD	EURJPY	EURUSD	GBPUSD	NZDUSD	USDCAD	USDCHF	USDJPY	
AUDUSD	100	81.6	-2.6	68.9	82.5	-79.3	-15.6	64.9	AUDUSD
EURJPY	81.6	100	11.7	81.8	54.2	-43.3	-26.1	68.5	EURJPY
EURUSD	-2.6	11.7	100	14.3	15.9	3.1	-86.2	-64.3	EURUSD
GBPUSD	68.9	81.8	14.3	100	38.2	-29.7	-36.2	52.7	GBPUSD
NZDUSD	82.5	54.2	15.9	38.2	100	-85.2	-34.1	30.2	NZDUSD
USDCAD	-79.3	-43.3	3.1	-29.7	-85.2	100	8	-35.6	USDCAD
USDCHF	-15.6	-26.1	-86.2	-36.2	-34.1	8	100	43	USDCHF
USDJPY	64.9	68.5	-64.3	52.7	30.2	-35.6	43	100	USDJPY
	AUDUSD	EURJPY	EURUSD	GBPUSD	NZDUSD	USDCAD	USDCHF	USDJPY	

Table 12 - Source: Investing.com

The correlation may change over time, which calls for a constant evaluation. For example, we can see a negative correlation between the EUR/USD cross and the USD/CHF. This means that a trader could buy the Fiber, while shorting the Swissy, allowing to reduce the risk. The table shows that it would make no sense to hedge the Fiber with the Loonie. Once we have analyzed the most important principle of money management, it is now time to study the differences between the martingale trading systems and the anti-martingale systems. The martingale systems add a new position of the same sign, to a losing trade. On the other hand, the anti-martingale systems add a new position of the same sign, to a profitable position. The *standard martingale* system takes profit on winners, doubling the exposure on losing trades; simply put, there is a high risk that losses could run up exponentially. The reverse martingale or "anti-martingale", does the exact opposite. It *closes losing trades*, and *doubles the profitable ones*. The answer to the question "which system is the most profitable" depends on the kind of market conditions. In particular, the s*tandard martingale works better in flat, range bound markets, while the anti-martingale performs better with volatile, trending markets.*

In conclusion, before placing an order in the market a trader should always know whether to adopt a classic strategy of money management or a hedging trading strategy, being fully aware of the risks and the benefits involved in both strategies. It is important to add that statistically the currencies tend to move in the range about 70 percent of the time. This means that applying a grid trading strategy might be profitable, but only under the condition that a trader is able to close the open losing trades promptly and to accept the loss in the event that the couple starts moving in a directional way. It should also be recalled that there are no specific rules in the positioning of the stop loss. Some of the greatest traders ever use very large stop loss, thus avoiding being stopped out for a simple retracing.

Holy Grail rule number 18:

Finally, we know where the Holy Grail is. *The money management along with the fundamental analysis are the keys we have been looking for to open the door where the legendary cup is.* Even the best indicators cannot avoid a loss. But *how a trader manage the losing trade is what can make him the* **CHOSEN TEMPLAR**.

Only the worthy can find the Grail, Leigh. You told me that.

Akiva Goldsman, for the film *The Da Vinci Code* (2006) based
on *The Da Vinci Code* (2003)

21. Conclusions

"Money doesn't always bring happiness. People with ten million dollars are no happier than people with nine million dollars!"- *Hobart Brown*

Over this journey in our quest for the Holy Grail of Forex we debunked several myths testing the pros and cons of different indicators and trading systems. Traders are often attracted by the "*charme*" of an indicator rather than by its proven ability to effectively interpret the markets. As Warren Buffett pointed out, it is always best to not fall in love with an indicator but rather be able to understand what is happening in the market at any given time. In other words, the fundamental analysis is essential to have a strong performance. If an increase in the interest rate is foreseen in a stable economy like the USA's, the USD might be expected to get stronger against other currencies. In other words, it would not be logical to short the US Dollar. It is good to remember that is not the interest rate applied by the central bank, but the expectations on it, that move the currency in a particular direction. It is also important to understand what is the current prevailing sentiment in the market. In times of high volatility and falling markets, the US Dollar and the Japanese Yen tend to be regarded as a safe haven, and consequently they tend to appreciate. A trader should then be always aware of the expectations on the interest rate of the countries of the underlying currency, the general conditions of the country and the sentiment that the big investors might have about the country under analysis. Once this initial assessment is done, it is then time to analyze the COT report; this way the trader has a real-time overview on the long or short positions that large investors hold. In the end, a trader can trigger a trade using the price action or by analyzing the Bollinger Bands when the volatility is higher than the average of the last periods. On the other hand, counter-trend trades will be opened when the volatility is low and when the trend of the underlying currency pair is uncertain. One should never open counter-trend trades when the underlying trend is clearly upward or downward. The trend should be always detected on the daily, weekly or monthly time-frames and the key is to not open a trade on the basis of a short time frame.

ALL RIGHT, TEMPLARS, FOR NOW THIS IS EVERYTHING YOU NEED TO KNOW. OPEN THE DOORS AND BASK IN THE LIGHT POURING OUT OF THAT MYSTERIOUS RELIC WHICH STANDS BEFORE YOUR VERY EYES.

Ad Maiora.

17847518R00080

Printed in Great Britain
by Amazon